MW00856739

In One Room

Stories from a Prairie School

(COVER)

By

Elizabeth M. Doherty

Illustrations by Della Conroy

Bless our Memories!
Betty Doherty

Copyright © 2023 by – Elizabeth Doherty – All Rights Reserved.

It is not legal to reproduce, duplicate, or transmit any part of this document in either electronic means or printed format. Recording of this publication is strictly prohibited.

Dedication

To my grandmother, Marie Kalkman Kent, who believed in the power of education. My grandmother was a lover of words and of children; she was comforted by poetry, the woods, and her own family. Inspired by the difficult decisions she made in her life to bring education to the students at the school and to her own children, I wrote this book. It is her voice I hear.

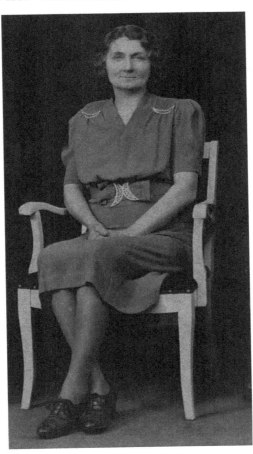

About the Author

Elizabeth M. Doherty was born and raised on her family's farm in west central Minnesota, second in a family of seven children. She has fond memories of growing up in Tara township and attending District 20, a one-room country school, her inspiration for this book.

Elizabeth graduated from high school in Benson, Minnesota. She attended the University of Minnesota, eventually earning a master's degree in social work. She began her career as a county social worker, but mid-career transitioned to a mental health therapist focused on helping people with issues of grief and loss. She loved her co-workers and had many favorite memories of tall tales shared during lunch time.

Currently, Elizabeth lives in Fridley, Minnesota with Joyce and their cat Schuster. She enjoys playing cards with her grandchildren Lucy and Zoe, her niece Kelly, and her four sisters. She loves smart talk and laughter with friends, walking in her park by the Mississippi River accompanied by her favorite blue heron.

Elizabeth always thought she would write someday, but never imagined it would be at 75 and about her childhood years.

Table of Contents

Preface

District 20 schoolhouse approximately 1990

It was in the spring of 2020 two months into the Covid epidemic, I was scrolling through my Facebook account and was surprised to come upon a photograph of the old country school from my childhood. The caption read, "So how much money would it take to move this piece of history five miles?" The post, from Anne Schirmer, who spent her childhood on the farm next to ours, drew 29 comments.

This school was the place where I began my education. In 1953, I was an eager first grader, and by the year 1959 when the school closed, I was a seasoned sixth grader. Surprisingly, the thought that our country school might be destroyed was quite unsettling. I was flooded with memories of this loadstar of my childhood. What if I could buy the land from the township, raise the money to restore the school, and donate it to the county's historical society? Why not?

I started by writing to the Swift County historical society and asking: If I were to buy the school and raise funds for the restoration, would they assume ownership and maintain the school on an ongoing basis? The answer was clearly no. Insurance costs and the risk of vandalism were too high, and it was five miles from the nearest fire department.

Disappointed, I decided I would do it myself. I would buy the school and raise the funds to restore and maintain it. I could start with my many relatives, after all, if my grandmother had not decided to teach out in the middle of the prairie in 1905, none of us would exist. I counted about 30 relatives who might have some sentiment for the project, as my grandmother, my mother, and three aunts had taught there.

My main contact in the area was Amanda Klucas, my cousin Keith Kent's daughter. She was a member of the township board, and more importantly, her heart was into saving this icon of our past. It was June 14, 2020, when I drove out to the school, 140 miles across the prairie from Fridley, the Minneapolis suburb where I live. As I drove through the farmland, now green with corn, soybeans, wheat, and oats, I remembered the calm, steady feeling of the prairie, of being able to see forever.

Amanda and two other board members were there to greet me. The school was a forlorn remnant of times gone by. The township board had saved the building by shoring up the exterior with steel siding and the interior with plywood flooring and paneling. It had the look of a garage or a storage shed. Yet, somewhere within these barren walls, the bones of the school were still there, still standing season upon season to winter's brutal blast and summer's scorching heat, still holding on.

The American flag and the blackboards were still there. I thought of how many times I had pledged my allegiance to that flag and how many times I had practiced my arithmetic on the old blackboards.

After some discussion and a subsequent board meeting, it was agreed that the destruction of the building would be delayed for two years if I paid the insurance and raised the money to restore the building. Amanda arranged for us to meet with a local carpenter, who agreed and said he could restore the building, but the cost was well beyond what I had imagined.

Could I raise $25,000? Maybe, but a problem came up that I had not foreseen. The population of the township was now less than 100 people. A place that in my childhood had nourished large families on farms that provided for us was now replaced by commercial farms that virtually ran themselves. Who would make use of this school? My vision of art classes, quilt making, book clubs, and visits by school children was evaporating before my eyes. The place where I began my education now stood isolated and alone.

I decided to let go of my idea, but it wouldn't let go of me. What if I were to memorialize this icon with words, mine and the other students who were launched there? I remembered the dusty blackboards and the American flag standing sentry since the school closed 64 years ago. I thought of our many stories buried underneath the paneling and plywood. I thought the best way to save the school was to give voice to these stories, to find a way to free them from the container that held them.

And so, I began. I did research by visiting the state and county historical societies, pouring over old newspapers, and interviewing historians and former students. In spite of the years gone by, I was able to meet with a number of students now in their 70s and 80s whose memories the school still held. This book is our stories.

Chapter 1: History of District 20

Our school, District 20, the first schoolhouse in Tara Township, Swift County, Minnesota, was built in the summer of 1877. A little frame building with just three windows, the school was   known locally as The Duggan School, as the land had been donated by one of the first immigrants, William Duggan. The little building served as the district school for 18 years. In 1895, Charlie McGuire bought the old schoolhouse and moved it to his farm to be used as a grain shed. That same year, our present schoolhouse was built. (1)

I was struck by the importance of education to the early immigrants. The wood-frame schoolhouse was built before some of the immigrant's own homes were built. Patrick Langan and Patrick Freeman, for example, arrived in Tara township from Massachusetts in 1877 and lived in a sod hut the winter of 1877-78. (2)

On December 2nd, 1878, the County Board of Commissioners of Swift County granted a petition recognizing Tara to be an official town government. The original name for the township was Ridgeville because of the hilly nature of the area, but it was later changed to Tara in memory of the Hill of Tara, the home of Irish kings in County Meath, Ireland. (3)

The first organizational meeting of the township was held in the District 20 schoolhouse on December 21st, 1878. At that time, four school districts were designated with nine sections of land each. District 20 subsequently comprised the sections of land in the northeast quadrant of the township. (4)

The early immigrants to Tara were predominantly of Irish heritage who came to Minnesota from Ireland, some by way of New England and Canada. Immigrants also came from Belgium, England, and other Northern European Countries. All came in the hope of a better life. (5)

The Irish had suffered extreme hardship in their native land in the mid-19th century. At that time, the potato crop was infected with blight and rotted in the ground. Potatoes were the mainstay in the diets of the rural Irish, and over a million people died of starvation and related complications. (6)

Two million people emigrated from Ireland; 75% of the immigrants came to the U.S. Most of the Irish immigrants remained on the eastern seaboard working in the mines, mills, stone quarries, and as domestic servants. (7)

In 1876 in St. Paul, Minnesota, a Catholic Bishop, John Ireland, formed an alliance with a railroad magnate, James J. Hill, to form the Catholic Colonization Bureau. Bishop Ireland was interested in offering a better life for the Irish Catholics who were working long hours of back breaking menial labor and experiencing strong bias in the eastern cities. He wanted to develop a strong presence of the Catholic Church in central and western Minnesota. At the same time, James Hill was building a railroad from St. Paul to the west coast and needed settlements along the new railway line in order for the railroad to thrive and prosper.

The Catholic Colonization Bureau, under the direction of Bishop Ireland, contracted for a total of 369,000 acres of land in west-central and southwestern Minnesota. The land was being sold for $1.25 per acre, and most of it was sold within 2 years. (8)

The land had been acquired by the railroad from the federal government following an agreement with the Dakota tribe and the U.S. government in 1851 in the treaty of Traverse des Sioux. After years of fighting and being overwhelmed by the U.S. government, the Dakota tribe surrendered the land and were forcibly moved to reservations in exchange for annual annuity payments.

Ten years later, in 1861, after a crop failure and a harsh winter with poor hunting, the Dakota were starving. For years, government agents delayed making the annuity payments After many broken promises on the part of the U.S. Government, the Dakota rose up in an effort to recover their land. A bitter battle ensued, with loss of life on both sides. The Dakota was defeated and forced onto reservations in the Dakotas and Nebraska. (9)

In the end, The Dakota, who had inhabited these lands for over 7,000 years (10), surrendered their land in Tara township to the Irish, who also had been driven from their land after 5,000 years. I cannot fathom what it would be like to give up your heart's blood, your land, your place on earth, after thousands and thousands of years as the Dakota and Irish did.

This land is old, but our footprint on it is new. Most of the immigrants who held this land moved on within one or two generations, drawn to more economically predictable lives in the towns and the cities.

The school thrived from 1877 to 1959. After 82 years, barely a hair's breadth in the history of time, it was decided that country schools were no longer optimal for the students, and decisions were made to consolidate with the larger town schools that offered broader educational opportunities. We lost the heartbeat of the community. I am marked by my experience at the country school. I carry this experience with me in all that I am and all that I do in this life.

Chapter 2: My First Visit

I was five years old the first time I entered the school, visiting my sister Barbara who was in the first grade. The teacher, Miss Nagler, said I could come to school for "a practice day" before I started the following year. The school building loomed large before me as we trudged up the hill, but it was not as big as our St. Malachy's Church, which was the biggest building I had ever seen.

The school was a white, wood-frame structure with a gray roof. I could see two windows, one on either side of the front door. Many heads were at the windows to get a look at me. My stomach was doing flip-flops, scared and excited, trying to be brave. I could see the outdoor toilets north of the playground. Barb told me the closest toilet was for us, the girls, and that I should hang on to the edges if I needed to go so as not to fall into the hole. I asked her if she could come with me for the first time. She said she would ask the teacher.

We walked up the three cement steps to the entrance. The steps were high, but I could manage them, even while hanging on to my tablet and dinner bucket. As we entered the school, Miss Nagler welcomed me. She showed me a visitor's desk at the back of the room. It was small, for a first grader, and I had to squeeze in. I didn't mind that the front of the desk pushed against my belly a little. After all, I was fat, and that was my fault.

I looked around. There were three windows on each side of the room, and there were many pictures on the walls. Some were drawn by the students in art class, and others were in frames and looked serious. One was of a man with long white hair dressed like a girl. I later learned that it was George Washington, the father of our country. I wondered why he had to dress like that. In the front of the room were three blackboards with the alphabet written on green cards over the top.

On the other side was a table with small chairs and an oil burner stove. Above the table were maps that could be pulled down like window shades. One of the maps was of Minnesota, one was of North America, and the third one was of the whole world. The maps were exciting and magical; I couldn't wait until I was old enough to be able to pull them down and look for places I could not imagine that I would ever visit.

Alongside the maps was a brick chimney with a black stove pipe sticking out that was attached to the oil burner stove. The stove would grumble and ping as it heated up, like it was tired of trying to keep us warm.

The floor was wood and kind of slippery. The school smelled like oil, wet wool, and old books with musty pages that crackled like Rice Krispies when I turned them. I liked the way the school smelled.

I didn't have to do anything; I could just watch. The teacher gave me a coloring book and colors, but I liked watching the big kids do their lessons at the front table with Miss Nagler. They knew a lot, and I couldn't imagine how I could learn all that.

I didn't have to go to the toilet until lunchtime, and Barb came with me. We shut the door and moved the wooden stick across, so it was locked. It was easy, and I didn't fall in. After school, we didn't have to walk home, Daddy was there waiting for us. We gave Lucy, Jean, and Pat a ride home. Daddy said, "Well did you learn anything?" I said no, but I had.

Chapter 3: First Day

On Tuesday, September 8th, 1953, I woke up excited; it was my first day of school. My mother had ordered a red and blue plaid shirt and blue jeans for me from the Montgomery Ward catalog. The pant legs were too long as I was quite round, my waist being wide and my legs short, but by rolling the pant legs up, the light blue denim inside was exposed, and I liked the look. I was ready for first grade. I could count to 100 and write my numbers to 10.

My father drove my sister Barb and me to school that day in our 1950 burgundy Ford sedan. The day was warm and smelled like silage as my father and uncles were chopping corn and filling our silo to feed the cows when winter came. Ordinarily, on such a fine day, we would walk the ¾ mile to school, south on the gravel road, and up the hill. But this day was special, it was my first day. We stopped to pick up the neighbor kids, Jean, Pat, and Lucy, who were already trudging up the hill and nearing the school. Pat climbed in the front with Barb and our father, and Jean and Lucy joined me in the back seat. I was thrilled to be in the back with the older girls. "Big first grader, huh?" Lucy said as she elbowed me in the ribs. I felt suddenly shy as I looked down at my new black shoes with silver buckles.

We got to school before the bell rang, and I was shown to my seat by our teacher, Mrs. Voorhees. My mother had been her teacher in the first grade, so I knew she must like me already. I checked to see where my sister Barb was sitting, just in case. I squeezed my round self into my first-grade desk directly behind Cynthia, the other first-grader. For the first time that day, my heart sank. Cynthia had a dress on! It was pale green with beautiful tiny checks, a grand pointed collar, and three round buttons marching down the front. I wore a dress only to church on Sundays.

We all stood for the pledge of allegiance, hand over heart, facing the flag. My sister Barb made sure I knew it. Then suddenly, our first-grade class was called up to the front of the room. "First-grade arithmetic," Mrs. Voorhees said solemnly. I slid out of my desk and walked to the front. Then, she asked us to go to the blackboard and write our numbers as far as we could. I proudly strode to the blackboard and wrote 1 through 10. I looked over at Cynthia, and she was in her 20s, then 30s, and on and on until 100! I was doomed! She was light years ahead of me. My face burned in shock and shame; Cynthia was a genius, and my life was over. I was sunk. Next, we were directed to sit down at the table, and the teacher showed us alphabet cards. I knew them A through Z! I perked up. We played a game; whoever said the letter first, got to put it in the pile in front of her. As I opened my mouth to say "A," Cynthia had already said it and placed the card in the space in front of her. We went on. Cynthia's pile grew. I captured the "G" and the "N" when Cynthia stopped to scratch a mosquito bite on her arm. We were dismissed, and I limped back to my seat. "Are you all right?" Mrs. Voorhees asked me. "I have a really sore foot," I said.

Chapter 4: Mornings

In September, October and May, and after the snow melted in April, we walked to school. In the winter months, we were driven to school in a carpool that included our neighbors, the Ollendicks and the Kepners.

On school days, Daddy would yell up the stairs to our bedrooms, announcing the time and the weather. He would call us each by name, starting with my oldest sister and on down the line to my youngest brother Pat. We were expected to answer. If you did not, your name would be called until you did. Pat had a hard time waking up, so his name would be called over and over. PAT! PAT! PAT! "For God's sake, Pat!" He would finally respond and say, "Yup." It was no use trying to fake a yup from Pat as our voices were well known to our father. Then we dressed, went downstairs, and sat at our places for breakfast. My father sat at the head of the table with Mike to his right and Pat to his left. My mother was next to Pat, then Eileen at her left. Barb was at the foot of the table with me on her left, followed by Helen. After Sharon was born, she sat in her highchair between Mama and Eileen.

For breakfast, we had Rice Krispies or Cornflakes, and toast with jelly or peanut butter, and we each got half an orange. When it was very cold, we had oatmeal or eggs. Sometimes on Saturdays, we had pancakes or French toast. I loved Saturdays.

We had 10 minutes to gobble down our breakfast and be out the door. While we ate breakfast, my mother packed our dinner buckets with bologna sandwiches, apples, and cookies. Then my father would look out the door and say, "There goes Jean and Pat." That was our signal to hurry out the door and rush to catch up with them before they got to Ollendicks' driveway. I could never catch Jean; she walked fast with her head down and did not fool around. She would be over the hill and out of sight by the time I was out of the driveway and on the road.

We had to make it to the school before the bell rang, or we would be tardy. Sometimes Miss Reardon would keep ringing the bell if she saw us at the top of the hill. We would not get a tardy mark on our report cards if we were there before the bell stopped ringing. We were usually the last ones to arrive.

Chapter 5: School Day

Left to right:
Front Row: Helen Doherty, David Smith, Eugene Smith, Peter Ollendick, Keith Kent, Ron Kent, Mike Doherty
Middle Row: Caroline Kaehler, Shirley Smith, Betty Doherty, Cynthia Buyck, Pat Kepner
Back Row: Lucy Ollendick, Katherine Andersen, Barb Doherty, Mary Andersen

A school day began with the pledge of allegiance. We all stood beside our desks, turned and faced the American flag, and recited the pledge. Under no circumstances was the pledge ever skipped, and there was no fooling around, period.

There were the regular subjects: arithmetic, and language, which included reading, writing, and spelling. Depending on your grade, you might have history, geography, or social studies. Then there were once-a-week subjects: art, music, and health.

The teacher called each grade to the front table for each subject. When it wasn't your turn at the table, you did worksheets, or practiced your reading and writing in preparation for your class to be called. In truth, most of us listened to all the other classes and learned by repetition.

The school began at 9, with lunch at 12, recess at 2, and dismissal at 3:30. For most kids, recess was the best part of the school day. It was a time for sports, games, and being able to yell and run free. For me, it was the most stressful event of the day. I was round, uncoordinated, and nearsighted, far from being athletic.

When the teacher announced "lunchtime" at noon we would get up from our desks and retrieve our dinner buckets from the cloakroom. We ate at our desks and were allowed to talk with our neighbors and even trade food if we wanted. After lunch, the teacher read to us to help us settle down and focus for the afternoon. I loved reading time and wished it would never end. My favorite books were the Laura Ingalls Wilder series, and I was enthralled by the exploits of Laura and Mary, Pa, Ma, and baby Carrie.

Fridays were the best because we had Art or Music. We sang from The Golden Book of Favorite songs, published in 1923. The books were quite battle-worn with fraying spines, and time-worn pages; the cover that had once been yellow was now mostly gray interspersed with yellow splotches. By second grade, I had memorized every song in the book and belted them out decidedly off-key. The teacher chose the music, which I did not question. In those days, the teacher was considered, like a priest or a doctor, infallible.

When she said, 'Let's sing My Grandfather's Clock,' it felt like my birthday or Christmas; the world shone with a light that came from somewhere else. I held in my mind a vivid picture of the clock, tall, elegant, and imposing, carved from the finest mahogany, tolling the grandfather's death. Other favorites we sang were, 'The Church in the Wild Wood' and 'My Home's in Montana,' which brought us to giggles thinking of Bill Wetzel, Miss Reardon's sweetheart who lived in Montana. We imagined him wearing silver spurs and riding a gray pony.

From early November until Christmas, we practiced our songs in preparation for the Christmas program. We had no piano or organ in the school and no musical training, but what we lacked in harmony, we made up for in enthusiasm.

Chapter 6: Water

    We had a rust-red handled pump outside, mounted on a wooden platform to the left of the swings. Pumping water was hard work, and it was even worse in the winter. Inside the school, near the front door on a small wooden table sat a white enamel pail. It had a few black spots on it where the paint was chipped off. Pumping the water required power pumping mightily and endlessly until a slight stream of water would spill out. Encouraged, harder pumping would produce a full stream. If you filled the pail too full so as not to have to pump another one later, the water would splash on your pant leg and freeze your pants before you got back into the school.

Our pail had a long-handled dipper hooked on the side. When you were thirsty, you asked the teacher's permission to leave your desk for a drink of water. You walked over to the water pail, unhooked the dipper, dunked it into the water, and had a drink. We all used the same dipper.

When Cynthia and I were in the 6th grade, and were the oldest girls in the school, we convinced the teacher that pumping and carrying water was boy's work. From then on, the 5th-grade boys were permanently assigned to water duty. We took on the job of washing hands before lunch. The students lined up by grade, first grade first. Each student held their hands over the enamel basin while Cynthia poured a half dipper of water. I handed them the bar of Palmolive soap. The student soaped up, then Cynthia poured the remaining half dipper of water over the hands, followed by me handing them a paper towel. The student vigorously wiped their hands on the sandpapery brown paper towel and tossed it in the wastebasket stationed close by. We could do 20 pairs of hands in 10 minutes. It might have been a world hand-washing record! I loved the job; hand washing is such a lonely occupation these days.

The toilets were another story. There were two tiny buildings at the north edge of the property, painted and shingled to be replicas of the schoolhouse; the one on the right was for girls, and the other on the left was for boys. Each toilet had a bench with two holes for doing your business. Looking down into the holes was not recommended. In winter, you needed to plan ahead. Going out to the toilet required putting on your overshoes and coat and trudging through the snow to get there. If you were the first one that day, you might have to stomp a path through the snow and brush the snow off the toilet seat before sitting down. Because we were modern, we had real toilet paper. In the early grades, if you had a small butt, the fear of falling in the toilet hole was real. It was important to learn to hang on to either side to prevent any such mishap.

Chapter 7: Pearl

Pearl Buyck made a bid of $77.77 to clean the school once a month during the 9 months the school was in session. She washed the windows, scrubbed the floors, cleaned the desks, and dusted the bookcases. I believe she polished the globe, too, as it seemed shinier after she had been there. She was the mother of my classmate Cynthia, the single other student in my grade, my best friend and arch-nemesis.

Pearl was clever enough to underbid the other mothers as she was a college graduate (the only one I knew). When I learned the word "precise" in language class, I thought of Pearl. She had good diction and grammar; her lips went tight across her mouth as she formed the correct words, well, precisely. Pearl was amazingly quick and had an economy of movement. She did not waste stuff, especially energy. She would have been a good shortstop. Her clothes had been worn a lot and were simply made; she was always clean, ironed, and neatly dressed.

Pearl and her husband, John, were trying to pay off the mortgage on their farm, and there was money for little else. They did not have plumbing in their house. Cynthia never wanted to pump the water at school, and I understand now that she was probably sick of it. From age 10, Cynthia ran the household: cooking, cleaning, and washing clothes and dishes. Pearl worked side by side with John in the field, clearing out rocks and tree roots. It wasn't great land, but it was the only kind of land they could afford. Pearl had a deep bronze tan that was sunburned over tan that didn't go away in the winter. Pearl was good-natured and had a laugh that went deep. She was an exotic person in my childhood world. She refused to become a Catholic and did not give up her religion when she married John. I knew she was going to hell for that, but I loved her anyway.

Chapter 8: Chores and Chickens

Left to right:
Front Row: David Smith, Bruce Kent, Tim Reardon, Helen Doherty
Back Row: Bob Peerboom, Mike Doherty, Ron Kent, Peter Ollendick, Keith Kent

Chores were an everyday expectation for us, whether in school or at home.

During the school term, Pearl was in charge of cleaning the school every month. Between monthly cleanings by Pearl, the teacher was responsible for the upkeep of the school with our help. My favorite chore was pounding the erasers, probably the best job. Typically, these were chores for first and second grade students. To pound the erasers, the student needed to collect the erasers from the trays under the blackboards and then was allowed to go outside and slam them vigorously against the steps. It caused a great energy release, so fun and so easy.

A rare chore involved cleaning up after accidents, like peeing or vomiting. Most of the teachers did the clean-up after these misfortunes, but one teacher was horrified at such a task and assigned it to the person who had the accident. She would retreat to the farthest corner and shout directions for the sweeping compound, broom and bucket. If it was a little child, a compassionate older girl typically helped.

Most of the students also had chores to do at home after school. Typical jobs included milking the cows, feeding and watering the animals. Most often, I got chicken duty that included feeding, watering, and gathering the eggs from the chickens. We then washed and packed the eggs to take into town to be sold at Baumgartner's, the local egg market. The egg money paid for our school clothes, shoes, and supplies, so we had to do it right.

In most of the year, chicken duty was not difficult, but in the winter, watering the chickens meant carrying pails of water from the barn to the chicken coop, which was a football field's distance away. I usually carried two pails of water which was a little too heavy for my 10-year-old arms, but that way I only had to make one trip. The pails would bang against my legs, splashing water as I tried to walk as fast as I could to end the misery. If it was cold, my pants legs would freeze, and with aching arms and frozen pants, I would enter the chickens' domain. The chickens would look at me peculiarly, and with squawks that sounded like questions, they would watch me fill their waterers.

Next came the egg gathering. The nests, with straw inside, were in cubby holes on the back wall. Some of the nests had eggs but no chicken, which meant easy picking. But then there would be the nasty hatching hen guarding her eggs. She did not want to give up her eggs, as she was planning on raising a family. This is how the battle began. If I tried to reach under her to get the eggs, she would come at me, pecking my hand like a machine gun while I fell back. I charged again, and this time I used diversionary tactics. I distracted her by poking her with a stick in my right hand, while I reached in with my left hand and grabbed her eggs. The rest of the egg gathering was uneventful. No blood was shed. A success.

To begin with, I did not hate the chickens. In the spring, my mother would clean their house before they arrived. The baby chick's house, known as the brooder house, was a Quonset-shaped shed across the farmyard from the garage.

It had windows on each side of the door for ventilation, and was painted red with a gray asphalt roof. My mother would shovel out the old straw and chicken poop and sweep and scrub the floor with hilex bleach. Then, she would spread the now spanking clean floor with peanut shells. Next, she would scrub the waterers and feeders, wipe them down with hilex bleach, and the brooder house was finally ready for its new occupants. The chicks arrived in boxes that resembled huge pizza containers with holes in them, 50 chicks per box. We always got 4 boxes. We carefully opened the lids of the boxes, and 50 balls of yellow fluff would be peering out at us. Peeping out of tune, they sounded like an orchestra string section gone mad. I adored them, for a while. I did not mind feeding and watering them until they lost their downy fluff and got ugly, taking on the appearance of balding white pigeons.

The chicks lived in the brooder house until fall, but over the summer, most of the roosters disappeared. My mother would execute them with a hatchet. We ate two roosters for Sunday dinner most weeks, except in hunting season when, with any luck at all, we would have pheasant. I did not mind the rooster killing; there was a measure of brutality to farm life that I accepted without question.

In the fall, it was time to replace the old hens in the chicken house with the new hens we called pullets. (Probably from the French word "poulet," which means young chicken). The pullets would be more productive egg-layers than the old hens, who would be shipped off to be made into soup.

The chicken swap would happen in the fall, after dark. A mysterious truck would appear, open in the back, filled with chicken crates. The crates would be unloaded off the truck and stacked on the ground. The whole family would be involved in this enterprise. We would raid the chicken coop, abduct the chickens from their roosts, and stuff them into the crates. At the age of 10, I could carry two chickens, one in each hand, holding on to one leg, suspended upside down. They squawked and tried to bite me, but I had on gloves. Over the summer, some chickens would have escaped and would be nesting in the trees, and we had to capture them too. My father devised a snare by bending the end of a wire into a hook, then he could sneak up, grab the sleeping chicken by the leg, and that was it for that chicken. I was in awe of my father's hands; he could carry eight chickens at one time, with a chicken leg wedged between each of his fingers and thumb. When all the chickens were captured and stuffed in the crates, my father and the driver loaded the chickens into the truck, never to be seen again. The next day my father cleaned out the chicken house and put in new straw, and we captured the pullets and carried them across the farmyard to their new home.

Chapter 9: The Dinner Bucket

I had a royal blue dinner bucket, square, with a black handle. It may have had a thermos that went inside, but I don't remember that. Typically, lunch was a bologna sandwich on homemade bread, an apple or a banana, and a chocolate chip cookie. On very good days, we had apple pie in a triangular plastic container or cake left over from someone's birthday, wrapped in plastic. Most of the frosting would stick to the plastic, so it was necessary to lick it off with as much grace as one could muster. I liked my dinner bucket, but I loved my sister Barb's. It was green with metallic stripes on the sides, a true work of art. We must have each chosen the one we wanted, but I typically chose one and then wanted the other.

I remember one incident with my dinner bucket. I overheard Lucy and Cynthia whispering about a teacher's pet, and my name came up. I was horrified at the thought, terrified of anything that would single me out as different from my classmates. My head was roaring, and I felt hot and then cold. I calmed down by reading ahead in my Alice and Jerry book. Then, that very afternoon, I seized an opportunity to fall out of favor with my teacher, Miss Reardon. We were at the end of the school day at our desks, gathering our papers and pencils before heading to the cloak room for our coats. Preparing to leave was getting quite noisy, and Miss Reardon shouted, "Please don't slam your dinner buckets on your desks!" I picked up my blue dinner bucket, looked her straight in the eye, and slammed it down onto my desk with all my 7-year-old might. "Betty!" Miss Reardon shouted. "I said don't slam your dinner bucket, and you just did it!" I began to cry, tears streaming down my freckled, chubby cheeks. I wiped my nose on my shirt sleeve. Miss Reardon got up from her desk, led me into the cloak room, and put her arms around me. I felt her soft cheek against my wet one. "Oh, Betty," she said, "I'm so sorry I yelled at you, but you just disobeyed me!" Hugged by the teacher! My plan had backfired; I was doomed. As I slunk back to my seat, all eyes were on me. It would be a long walk home.

Chapter 10: The Plum Trees

Behind the schoolhouse were the plum trees, and the magical kingdom that was held inside. The trees were old and bent, and their branches and trunks formed a hollow where we girls gathered for secret meetings to drink imaginary tea, and build milkweed pod dolls. In the spring, when the trees were bursting with white blossoms, we made plum-blossom headdresses. The hollow formed by the plum trees was the most wonderful place I have ever been, filled with secret alliances and lessons from older, wiser girls.

On our farm, we did not have plum trees. We had only spindly, newly planted cottonwood trees that were unfit for secret gatherings. Trees did not exist on the prairie except along creeks and rivers, and where they were planted around homesteads to break the wind.

Someone planted those plum trees behind our schoolhouse long ago. I've decided to think it was my grandmother, who taught at our school in 1905. She must have missed the woods of her home and, looking out, she saw only an ocean of grassland that went on relentlessly, for miles upon miles. Perhaps, my grandmother thought a grove of plum trees would give her eyes some comfort as she looked out. The smell of the blossoms in the spring would be intoxicating, bringing her back to her childhood days. Or maybe she thought it would be good for her students to know about trees and plums and shelter from the endless wind that they provided.

The plum trees have been gone a long time, as has my grandmother, but I know somehow that she taught me to love trees and plums and secret hiding places. Like her, I love words and putting them together in ways that feel like music. Like her, I know that a poem can lift you from the dark. I wish I could tell her now that she made a difference in my life, that she mattered and that her memory is alive in me.

Chapter 11: School Nurse

Twice a year, in the fall and in the spring, the county nurse came to our school to check us over. She was a tall, thin woman with gray hair. I remember her as being erect in posture, and when she sat, she perched her butt on the edge of the chair, prim and smiling. Her smile was a fake smile, like the Cheshire Cat. I thought she was probably about 100 years old, and I hated her. There was one particular year that I specifically remember her visit.

The county nurse's main job was to check our weight. She brought the scale with her; I don't know how she got the heavy scale up the steps and into the school, but she did. It was the kind with the numbers across the top, and you moved the weight across the numbers until it balanced with the weight on the opposite side. We lined up by grade, starting with first grade. As each child stepped on the scale, she shouted the child's weight across the room to our teacher, who wrote it in a small book with a brown cover.

I dreaded county nurse days. I was a fat kid and was ashamed of my weight and didn't want the teacher and the other kids to know. As the line in front of me got shorter, I could feel my cheeks burning red. There was no way out. I stepped on the scale. "122 pounds," she bellowed at Mrs. Suter, the teacher. I was 10 years old, and I weighed 122 pounds. Cynthia, my classmate, weighed 78 pounds. I was numb with shame. I went back to my desk and stared at my hands. At recess, I could hear giggling from over by the swings, I knew they were laughing at me. I felt tears in my eyes, but they did not come down my face. Somehow, I walked home.

"How was school?" my mom asked from the kitchen sink. "The county nurse came today," I said. My mom turned around and looked at me with sad eyes. She knew. "Do you want to help me set the table?" she asked. "OK," I said and got the plates down from the cupboard.

Chapter 12: Saddle Shoes

In the second grade, I got a new pair of saddle shoes. They were brown and white with rust-colored soles; they were the finest shoes I had ever owned. I was so excited to walk into school with them that I decided I would not say a word until someone noticed. I walked faster that morning on my trek to school because I couldn't wait to get there. I noticed as we passed Ollendicks' that my feet were feeling a little sore and that my shoes were rubbing against my heels. I remember my mother had said, "It takes a while to break in new shoes." My feet were quite sore when I got to school, but I didn't notice as three girls said they liked my shoes. Lucy even said so, and she was in the 6th grade. It was a good day at school, we had art class and got to use real paints and paintbrushes to paint what we could see from our desks. I painted a picture of the flag, but I couldn't keep the red and white stripes from running together. In the end, it really didn't look much like a flag. Miss Reardon said it was good that I didn't get much paint on my desk. When school was over at 3:30, I picked up my sweater and dinner bucket from the cloakroom and headed out the door. By the time we got to the hill, my heels were very sore, and each step was painful. I had to tell my older sister Barb that my new shoes hurt my feet. She was nice and said she'd carry my dinner pail and worksheets. By the time we got to Ollendicks' driveway, there was blood on my heels and inside my new shoes. I had to take my shoes off. It hurt to walk home on the gravel road, but after a while, I found a smooth track down the right side of the road. My white socks were black when I got home. My mother said I'd better wear my old shoes for a while until we could go to town and have the heels stretched.

Chapter 13: Kitten Ball

The hands-down favorite game played at recess in our country school was kitten ball. It was the same game as softball, but in our part of the country, it was called kitten ball. Apparently, a Minneapolis fire department first called the game Kitten Ball in 1895, having named their team the Kittens. (11)

We usually had about 16 students in grades 1-8, with 8 students on each team. First, the teacher picked the captains. Next, a bat was tossed in the air, and one of the captains grabbed the bat. The captains then went hand over hand on the bat and the last hand to fit three fingers onto the neck of the bat chose the first player. The big boys were chosen first, then the athletic girls. Next came the smaller boys, the smaller girls, and then me. I was chosen last because I was the worst player, I typically struck out when at bat. I couldn't catch either a fly ball or a grounder and was the slowest runner. I was round, uncoordinated and nearsighted. Each time I came up to bat, the infield came closer to the home plate, knowing I couldn't get it over their heads. One day, I hit the ball hard. I could feel the sting of the bat in my hands as it collided with the ball. It made a crack as the ball flew out past 2nd base! I ran for first base with everything I had. I got there before Pat Kepner was able to throw it in from behind second base. I was safe! My team cheered, our opponents were incredulous. Next up was the top of the batting order, Kenny Kaehler! The agreed-upon rule for Kenny was he had to bat with one hand because he typically hit the ball across the road and into the ditch on the other side. We couldn't afford to lose any more balls in the tall grass of the ditches. He hit the first pitch across the road one-handed. I ran for second base as he was loping along behind me and gaining on me as I reached second. "Hurry up, Betty. He's going to run you over!" Lucy shouted. Kenny was right behind me as I ran for third base. He put his hand on my sweaty back, grabbed my shirt, and pushed me in front of him across home plate. I scored! Maybe I won't be picked last next time.

Chapter 14: Gophers

There were two kinds of gophers that continually plagued us in the schoolyard, in our house yards, and in our fields. The first kind of gopher was the generic gopher, who was known technically as a "thirteen-lined ground squirrel." These characters dug holes and burrowed systems of underground tunnels. The holes were dangerous underfoot, causing multiple occurrences of twisted but rarely broken ankles. Gopher hunting was a popular activity for young boys and their dogs. The hunt required finding the second, or "back door," of the gophers' hideout. Then, buckets of water were carried over to the hole and poured in. The gopher was then forced to run out of the "front door" or risk drowning. When the wet gopher ran out, he was captured by the dog, or by the boy with a twine string noose around the hole or with a baseball bat and swiftly executed.

The second kind was the pocket gopher. These guys made mounds easily a foot high in the farm fields. Their biggest danger was in wrecking farm machinery and eating budding corn and soybean crops. The pocket gophers were large and furry, twice the size of the ground squirrels. The township established a bounty on pocket gophers: 22 cents for the two back feet of the gopher. The feet needed to be presented to the township bounty officer, who was my father. Farmers and their sons would trap the pocket gophers, kill them, remove their back feet, and bring them to my father to collect their bounty. Often my father was not home, and my siblings and I had to pay the bounty. Most often, gopher-hunters collected the feet and stored them in a large coffee can. When the can was full, it would be brought to our farm for counting. Foot counting was a most dreaded job. The readers will be spared the details of this operation for the sake of decency. All the school children knew that our family bought gopher feet, but it was a puzzle as to what we did with them.

On our farms, lives were taken, as a matter of fact, to protect us and our livelihood, to feed us, and to help us hold on.

Chapter 15: The Christmas Program

Getting ready for the Christmas program was the highlight of each school year. We began by stringing wire from the hooks that were permanently screwed into the ceiling. The wires sectioned the front quarter of the room into three spaces. The dressing room on the right was for the girls, and the dressing room on the left was for the boys. The stage was in the middle. We attached bed sheets that had been dyed dark blue to the wires with large safety pins to mark the spaces. The front of the stage had sheets on either side that could be pulled back and forth to open and close between acts. It was a time of major excitement!

Each grade performed an act, and we all sang a Christmas carol   together for the opening number and for the grand finale. Each year I hoped for a major role in the production, but it never happened. My biggest role was behind the scenes. As a 6th grader, I was given the assignment of overseeing the girls' dressing room. I was to stifle nervous giggles and loud whispering as well as try to prevent the girls from jumping up and down, bumping into the curtain like a sack of kittens, when the excitement became unbearable. I took my job seriously and kept them in line like a supreme commander.

The audience sat on folding chairs, coats were stacked on the teacher's desk, and overshoes dripped wet snow on the floor. We could hear the murmur of good-natured conversation while we waited behind the curtain for the program to begin. At 7 pm, the curtain was pulled back. Hardly anyone forgot his/her lines, and the one-act plays went off without a hitch. The props came and went off the stage seamlessly, and no one tripped or forgot to close the curtains. The audience roared with applause after each act. As the curtain was pulled after the last song, we piled out from behind the curtain and took our final bow. We were stars bursting with pride and happiness.

Afterward, we gathered for Kool-Aid, coffee, and Christmas sweets. Each mother brought her best-baked desserts, brownies, decorated Christmas cookies, and Rice Krispies dyed green and sprinkled with red hots. Afterward we sang carols with the audience, finishing with Silent Night. As we drove home, stuffed with desserts and stuffed all together in our 1950 Ford, I knew this was the best night of my life.

Chapter 16: The Picnic

The Friday before Memorial Day, the last day of school, was the school picnic. Next to the day of the Christmas program, it was the most exciting and joyous school day.

Picnic tables were made in the schoolyard by the fathers; sawhorses were covered with 8-foot-long wooden planks. If it had rained a lot in the spring and the corn was not planted, our fathers needed to stay at home and finish the planting. Our mothers would then have to make the picnic tables. They would lift the heavy planks up on the sawhorses with one mother on each end. Our mothers then covered the raw plank tables with brightly colored tablecloths. The tables were laden with every family's favorite dish, potato salads, fried chicken, baked beans, and sweets of every description. Kool-Aid was there for the taking. I loved food and managed to try nearly everything, including as many sweets as I could load on my plate. This one special day, my mother looked the other way.

Sadly, this day was also field day, which was torture for me. Races of all kinds were made ready to happen, followed by a massive kittenball game where even the fathers played. With much laughter, the fathers made the game exciting by hitting the ball hard and huffing and puffing around the bases.

I dreaded the races and tried to creatively come up with reasons for being unable to participate. Perhaps, I stepped in a gopher hole and sprained my ankle remembering to limp carefully. Other reasons I used were that I had a stomach ache (often true), a headache, or that my shoes were too tight. My mother and the teacher knew I did not want to be embarrassed by trailing far behind in the races, so I was often given a pass.

After the races and the kittenball game came the biggest event of all, the report cards. We would find out if we passed or failed. I had no idea the report cards were based on school performance. I thought it was simply based on the whim of the teacher at the moment. My hands shook as I opened the brown envelope and looked at the pink card. Passed! I was safe for another year.

Chapter 17: Marching

It was a cold, wild and windy day. The house moaned and cracked in its efforts to hold back the blowing snow as the blizzard tried to push in the windows. The furnace thundered and blew hard against the heat registers. Thundering, too, was my father, who called us to get up. "Dress warm. It's 40 below!" he yelled up the stairs. I crawled out of my blankets and quickly tried to put on my underwear and my jeans with the plaid flannel linings. It was too cold to shiver.

I hurried down the stairs for the egg, toast, and jelly my mother had ready for us. While my dad warmed up the Ford, my brother, sisters, and I threw on our wool jackets, scarves, hats, and rubber boots and scrambled frantically to find our mittens. Then, we headed out to hop into the Ford and travel to school. The tires shattered the snow like breaking glass as we drove out of the driveway and turned left on the gravel road leading up to the school. As we neared the school, I noticed there was no smoke coming out from the chimney. The pilot light must have gone out on the oil-burning stove again. When we climbed the steps into the school, stomping the snow off our boots, we saw the teacher on her knees, trying to relight the pilot light. On the floor lay a pile of burned wooden matches from prior attempts. My father was able to light the pilot on his first try, and the stove roared and boomed into operation. We sat quietly at our desks, still wearing our boots, hats, and coats, waiting for what (I hoped) was sure would come next.

And then... the teacher said, "We need to keep warm until the building heats up. Why don't we do some marching?" This was turning out to be a perfect day! She took the 78 rpm record, from its sleeve, FAVORITE JOHN PHILLIPS SOUSA MARCHES BY THE UNITED STATES MARINE CORPS BAND. She carefully placed the record on the portable suitcase-shaped Motorola record player, gently touched the needle down onto the record, and we were marching! Unbridled joy flooded me as I marched proudly around the room. As the strains of "Stars and Stripes Forever" filled my ears, I was transformed into a soldier, turning my head toward the generals in the reviewing stand. "And we're done!" she would say, and it was over. Just like that.

Chapter 18: Potato Days

At the country school during the wintertime, when the temperature dropped below zero, the oil stove got hot. On cold winter days, the stove thundered and pinged nearly non-stop. Early on, we discovered that if you wrapped a potato in tin foil and put it on the stove in the morning, the potato would be perfectly baked by lunchtime. In my blue dinner bucket, I would be carrying the necessary sides: salt, pepper, and plenty of butter. During morning classes, the smell of roasting potatoes would grow stronger and stronger, so by noon, the hunger pangs would be distracting. There would be times when my mother would pack soup in our dinner bucket too, but the soup was a disappointment. A potato was the best. When lunchtime came, we would go out to the cloakroom to pick up our dinner buckets that were lined up on the shelf above our coats, and we'd put on our mittens, as the potatoes were too hot to touch. We'd select our potato from the row on the stove (mine had Betty carefully taped to the tin foil) and take it to our desks to be unwrapped. It was tricky to open the potato with mittens on. As I peeled back the tin foil, the steam would fog my glasses, and the aroma would be intoxicating. The next step was to take the spoon from my dinner bucket, stab the handle into the soft potato and cut it open. On went the butter, which formed yellow rivers on the tin foil beneath the potato, followed by salt and pepper. Each spoonful of potato and butter was glorious! I would carefully scrape all the potato from the skin and then eat the skin too. I did not talk much to anyone on potato days, as the whole potato project was quite absorbing, and I did not want to be asked for a bite. I felt sorry for my classmates with their sad sandwiches, but I could not spare one bite of my potato.

Chapter 19: The Blizzard

Minnesota winters are unpredictable, fierce, and relentless. Wind-whipped snowstorms dump mountains of snow upon the land, followed by sub-zero temperatures. The granddaddy of them all, however, is the blizzard. It is a rare Minnesota winter that does not provide several of them. According to the National Weather Service, a blizzard is defined as blowing and/or falling snow with winds of at least 35 mph, reducing visibility to a quarter of a mile or less for at least 3 hours.

We in Minnesota keep a list of the most deadly blizzards. Such storms last more than 3 days, bring at least 2 feet of snow, and have sustained winds of at least 50 mph. One of the worst in Minnesota's history was the blizzard of 1888. It was January 12th, and it started as a mild day, but an unexpected storm arrived, and the temperature dipped to nearly forty below zero. Thick snow blew and swirled. Because of the mild weather that morning, the children were unprepared for the storm. Hats, mittens, and overshoes were left behind and forgotten as children left their homes to walk to school. Many children died on their way home that day due to the extreme cold and zero visibility. The death toll was over 200 children. The storm became known as the "Children's blizzard" because so many lost their lives. (12)

Most prairie people have a healthy respect for blizzards, and there are few among us who have not had a harrowing experience. As powerful as a tornado, as strong as a hurricane, and as sudden as a flash of lightning, the fear of children being lost on their way home from school in a blizzard was grounded in the cruel reality of previous storms.

There was such a storm that brought fear and awe to our country school. Dim memories of this storm remain with Alice Peerboom and Donald Andersen, who were students at District 20 during this time. It was believed to have happened in the winter of 1950 when Marjorie Lageson was the teacher. The Minnesota DNR does state that the Blizzard of 1950 was one of the worst on record for the Northern plains. (13)

The day broke bitterly cold and sunny that morning, although the snow had stopped. Alice and Delores were reminded by their mother, Nina, to dress warmly as it was 28 degrees below zero. Ted, their father, blew in the kitchen door with a blast of frigid air as he stomped the snow off. "It's pretty deep out there," he announced, "over the top of my over shoes. I think I'll hitch up the horses, and we'd have better luck getting through the snow." Ted warmed his hands over the stove for a couple of minutes and then went back out to harness the horses.

The team was an old brown horse, Sammy, that Ted had since he got married, and a new black horse, Prince, that he picked up at the sale barn for a good price. The old horse, Sammy, slipped easily into the harness and sighed mightily at the prospect of hard work. The young horse, Prince, was excited about a new adventure and bounced around with great enthusiasm as Ted tried to get him into the harness. Ted had to take off his gloves to hook up the harness, and his hands were stiff with the cold. "Easy boy," he commanded in a stern voice that sometimes worked. Prince settled down for a minute, and Ted slipped on the harness. Ted hitched the horses to his sled, which was an old farm wagon with runners attached. Ted had replaced the wheels with runners to create a sled that was more useful in the winter. He wrestled his team up to the house to pick up the girls.

"We'd better get going," Ted said. Alice and Delores buttoned up their wool coats, put on their overshoes, scarves, and mittens, and were out the door with their father. The sun on the snow was blinding, and Alice covered her eyes with her mitten. Sammy put his head down and plowed through the snow while Prince pranced along, trying to pull Sammy to go faster. Back and forth, they struggled until they reached the schoolyard. "We could have walked faster," Alice shouted over the crunch of the snow and the clip of the horses' hooves. "I'll pick you up early if the wind picks up," Ted said as the girls started up the steps to the school.

Mrs. Lageson had her coat on when they opened the door and walked inside. "It's cold, girls," she said. "The stove went out last night, so you'll have to leave your coats on till it warms up." Mrs. Lageson put a marching record on the phonograph, turned it up loud, and they all marched round and round the room until they were warm and laughing from the fun of it. "Maybe we'll skip reading classes today, and I'll read to you from Laura Ingalls Wilder's "The Long Long Winter," Mrs. Lageson said. Everyone knew that this was a special day and thought it would be a good idea. Arithmetic and spelling classes could not be skipped, however, and everyone put their heads down and did their worksheets.

Rodger heard it first. The wind picked up suddenly, changing directions to the northwest, and snapped a large branch off the big cottonwood with a loud crack. Suddenly, the wind was roaring louder and louder. The snow was fresh and blew easily, and soon it would be a whiteout. Outside the school, cars were honking as the children hurried to get their coats on and ran out to meet their fathers. "Dad won't be able to come to get us in this weather," Delores said, and she started to cry. Mrs. Lageson's face turned white, and when she spoke, her voice came out tight and scratchy. "We will all be safe," she said.

Then, Alice heard Prince's high-pitched neigh. "They made it!" Alice said as she flew out the door toward the sleigh. "Put on your scarf!" Mrs. Lageson shouted from the door.

Most of the parents had picked up their children and were struggling through the deep snow to get home, but Donnie remained at school. His home was the farthest from school, and by now, the roads were impassable. A gust of wind came at 50 miles per hour and shook the schoolhouse, blowing out the pilot light on the stove. "Well, it will get too cold to stay here now," Mrs. Lageson's voice cracked. "When the wind lets up, we'll just have to walk over to my in-laws' place."

Julius and Amelia Lageson lived at the Regan farm just up the road, but they couldn't see the house through the blowing snow. The wind blew harder, and the schoolhouse shook and cracked. Donnie was worried but he felt safe with his teacher. And then, just as it came, it stopped. The sun came out, pale and small among the clouds. "We'll go now," Mrs. Lageson said, her voice stronger. She took Donnie's hand, and they struggled together through the snow, waist-deep at times for Donnie, until they reached the Lagesons' house. Donnie knew the farm; he stabled his horse Duke in the barn there when he rode his horse to school. Walking through the deep snow was hard work, and it was now 20 below zero. Mrs. Lageson and Donnie were both exhausted and ruddy-cheeked as they made it up the steps to the front porch. "My word!" Amelia said as she opened the door. "You poor dears!" She helped them out of their wet coats and sat them in front of the oil burner stove in the living room. That night they had beef soup with popcorn on it and told storm stories. Donnie slept with Julius, and Mrs. Lageson slept with Amelia. Julius snored, but Donnie fell asleep anyway, safe and warm. In the morning, they had pancakes, and after the snowplow went past, Donnie's father, Woody, came for him. As Woody stomped the snow off his boots on the porch and came inside, Donnie was just finishing his 5th pancake.

"Hi, Dad," he said, "I wasn't even scared!"

"Your mother was worried sick about you!" Woody said, "But we knew your teacher would keep you safe."

Chapter 20: Teachers

I loved and respected my teachers at District 20. They were young women with the energy and backbone to do what needed to be done in all the roles   expected of them. They were the teacher, the nurse, the custodian, the librarian, and the guidance counselor for all the children in first through eighth grades.

It has been reported that Nellie Knall was the first teacher when the school was established in 1877. There were no records for another 10 years. We have the names of the teachers until the school closed in 1959, except for the period from 1898 to 1904 when no records could be located. (See List of Teachers)

I have attempted to share stories of five of these teachers, beginning with my grandmother, Marie Kalkman Kent, who taught at District 20 in 1905, my mother, Mary Kent Doherty, who taught in 1943 and 1945, and Marjorie Regan Lageson, who taught from 1949-1952. I was able to interview Margaret Nagler Voorhees at her home, who taught at the school from 1952-1954, and I spoke with Jeanette Reardon Wetzel by telephone, who was our teacher from 1954-1956. Hopefully, the reader's imagination of the life of a country schoolteacher can be enlivened by the stories on these pages.

Chapter 21: Marie Kalkman Kent

In 1905, Marie Kalkman, my grandmother, came to teach at the country school in Tara township. She was 23 years old and had completed 9 months of teacher training at the Saint Cloud Normal School, which later evolved into St. Cloud State University.

Marie was born and raised near the small town of Clear Lake, Minnesota. Her father was a wealthy man who owned a successful granite business in the St. Cloud area. Marie was not needed to do housework as a child; she told me that she wandered the woods near her home and spent her time with books. It makes sense that she would want to become a teacher, but what would possess her to travel 100 miles from home at the turn of the century to teach on the prairie populated by struggling immigrants?

How Marie Kalkman landed in Tara township teaching at our country school is a mystery. No one is alive who knew her better than I did. Her children are all gone, so I can only speculate about her reasons. Perhaps she wanted an adventure? The idea of traveling alone out into the prairie by train, horse or buggy intrigued her. It may have been a romantic adventure in a predictable, stable life. Or perhaps she wanted to go where she was most needed, out into the prairie, where the children would need to learn about the magic of words and stories of the world beyond the prairie. I could find no hints in letters or a long-lost journal to inform me. Would she have come to Tara township if she knew what her life would be?

The schoolhouse Marie taught in was the same one that I attended 50 years later. I was grateful to discover that the story of the early days of District 20 was recounted in a publication of the Swift County Historical Society by Eva Boettcher, who taught in the school from 1945-1949. (14)

I learned that in the early years, perhaps in the early 1900s, the children walked to school around sloughs and through the grass as high as their heads. They burned wood in the stove that the big boys had chopped. The desks were homemade and double seaters. The school term was 4 months long; 2 months in the fall and 2 months in the spring. The students read from Appleton's Reader, which was only available up to the 5th grade. The children had slate boards with slate pencils for arithmetic and writing assignments. There was no library and no globe. At recess, children played ball and snared gophers with twine strings. The teacher's salary was $20 per month.

At 23, this is what Marie Kalkman found as she began teaching at the little country school. It was likely that she lived with one of the families in the district, a practice known as "boarding the teacher." She no doubt walked to school early in the morning to start the wood stove and prepare for the day's lessons. Her students were between the ages of 6 and 20, as there was no secondary school available. Some students stayed in school as long as they could until reaching age 21. I imagine she might have had the older children teach reading, arithmetic, and spelling to the younger ones, a method that remained in practice throughout the years at country schools.

I wonder which family she boarded with while she taught at the school. I'd like to imagine she stayed with Nell Kent, an unmarried woman who lived in a large house close to the school that she shared with her mother, Catherine, after the death of her father, James, in 1899. Nell's brother David, at age 22, may have been living in the Kent house.

David, my grandfather, was the man Marie would later marry, and afterward she no longer taught since married women were not permitted to teach. My grandfather was an Irish man, unlike her stern and stoic German father. David loved fun, played his fiddle, and laughed at the elaborate tricks he played on his neighbors. It was clear that my grandmother loved her husband; she called him David, never Dave, in a tone of deep respect and affection.

Together Marie and David had 6 sons and 3 daughters. They struggled to make a living, food at times was scarce, and farming the land was brutal and demanding. Marie was not prepared for such hardship. Early in their marriage, the washing machine broke. David only got around to getting it fixed years later, so Marie washed the clothes for a big farm family on a washboard in a large tub.

I remember a particular incident with my grandfather. He drove to our farm in his ancient, gray Chevy. As we sat in the farmyard visiting, the terrifying rooster that ruled the barnyard strutted by. We ran! Grandpa picked up his cane and smote him dead with one blow. "Tell your mother we are having chicken for dinner," he said.

In the first decade of the 20th century, Marie learned the backbreaking work of farm life. Growing huge gardens, putting up fruits and vegetables for the winter, and slaughtering chickens, cows, and pigs, were all part of what was required to keep your family going. The repeated everydayness of washing clothes, cooking, scrubbing floors, doing dishes, this was her life.

My earliest memory of my grandmother was of her stabbing open a tin can of peaches with a butcher knife. With each thrust, the can gave way a little more until she was able to peel off the jagged top with her fingers. Her hands were marked with purple scars from where she missed.

Against all odds, my grandmother was determined to send her 9 children to high school. My uncle Dick, the oldest, rode his horse through extremely bitter prairie winters 11 miles to Benson, Minnesota, where the high school was located. My Aunt Kit and my mother, who were 4th and 5th in the family, boarded in town and worked for their keep. Each year, when the next child completed country school, my grandfather would say, "Where's the money going to come from for high school?" My grandmother would say nothing and somehow, she patched it together to make high school happen.

My grandmother was the queen of hospitality; her table was full of family, friends, or whoever happened by at mealtimes. My mother told me that she would invite traveling salesmen to eat with the family if they were there at dinner time. Whatever she had, she shared. Sometimes, it was very little, but she made it stretch.

I remember my grandmother was vague, often appearing to be somewhere else. She would light up when we came to see her, and I could feel her love, but as years went by, she drifted, faded, and was less than present. I have come to believe that she was blunted by her life experiences.

I sensed that she longed for poetry, her books, and the woods. I never saw her angry, and I never saw her complain; she simply drifted further and further away. In the end, she had "hardening of the arteries" they said. Today we call it dementia. I think she just went home to her woods, her books, and her poetry.

Like her, I love words and putting them together in ways that feel like music. Like her, I know that a poem can lift you from the dark. I wish I could tell her now that she made a difference in my life and that her memory is alive in me.

Chapter 22: Mary Kent Doherty

I was proud that my mother taught at our country school and I love to hear her stories. She taught there in 1943 and again in 1945. I believe she taught in another country school in the area in 1944, but I never understood why teachers moved from one school to another. Three of my aunts taught at our school as well, and it seemed as though they all came and went, and I was never quite sure what it was that would draw them from one to another until I met with Margaret Voorhees, who taught at District 20 from 1952-1954. "The school board thought it important to expose the students to a variety of teachers, so moves occurred every two years", she said.

"It was wartime" Mama would say as if that explained everything. I didn't know what wartime was, as I had not lived through it, but I did know that she worried about her brothers who were away at war and that some things were rationed, like sugar and gas.

Mama smiled when she talked about being a teacher. "In 1945," she told me, "an exciting event happened at the school, electricity was installed." She went on to tell me about how fascinated the children were since so many did not have electricity in their homes. Of particular interest were the electrical outlets. Mama brought a radio from home and plugged it in. It took a while for the radio to warm up, but soon static could be heard. Mama turned the knob until music could clearly be heard. The children were ecstatic as the music played. "What would happen if we stuck a spoon in there?" Richie said, pointing to the slots in the outlet. "Don't ever do that!" Mama said, "you'll get a big electric shock." Richie, a third grader, said, "let's have Ray try it," referring to a very innocent first grader.

Mama loved words, and she wanted her students to love them too. In particular, she loved poetry and believed that it was important to memorize poems so you could recite them at times in your life when you needed them. Poetry was always an everyday part of my mother's life, as it was my grandmother's. She taught her pupils to memorize nursery rhymes as she believed the rhythm and the meter were important to learning everything else.

The friendly cow, all red and white,

I love her with all my heart.

She gives me cream with all her might,

To eat with apple tart.

She wanders lowing here and there,

And yet she does not stray,

All in the pleasant open air,

And the pleasant light of day.

And blown by all the winds that pass,

And wet by all the showers,

She walks among the meadow grass,

And eats the meadow flowers.

-Robert Louis Stevenson

One of her students, Don Andersen, told me that my mother, his first-grade teacher, was the best teacher he ever had. "Because of your mother," he said, "I learned to love reading."

Mama got her preparation to teach at St. Cloud Normal school. In 9 months, she could be certified to teach in a country school. She continued her education over the summers and earned the equivalent of a two-year degree. Like my grandmother, she believed education was the key to a richer life. "Education is not something anyone can take from you," she said. "You will always have it." I don't remember her tying it to success in terms of financial advancement or professional status, but rather as the wealth of a developed mind.

When I started school, my first-grade teacher, Mrs. Voorhees, had been my mother's student when she was in the first grade. I certainly thought that would give me a leg up, but she seemed unreasonably fair when it came to my classmate Cynthia and me. To my disappointment, she treated us equally and gave me no second chances when it came to collecting flashcards or learning spelling words.

I was afraid to ask Mrs. Voorhees what it was like having my mother as a teacher. Then, one-night she could not make it home because the roads were impassable during a blizzard. She came to stay overnight at our house. I was equally proud and horrified that the teacher would be at our house overnight. It was decided that she would sleep in the little girl's bedroom, evicting Helen to the couch for the evening. After she spent some time in her room getting situated, Mrs. Voorhees returned to the kitchen to join us. She sat on our red metal kitchen stool that had two folding steps and visited with my mother while she made supper.

That red metal stool was for Pat to sit on at the kitchen table after Eileen, the new baby, had deposed him from the highchair. I wondered if Mrs. Voorhees would give the stool to Pat when it was time to eat. I was embarrassed that she had taken off her shoes and had her stocking feet perched on the folding steps of the stool. I had never seen her unshod feet before. What if she took off her socks? I was entranced by this scene. Would I get up the courage to ask her what it was like having my mother for a teacher? My mother turned over the hamburgers in the pan producing a loud sizzle. As I was considering how I could ask her, my sister Barb said, "What was it like having my mother for a teacher?" She stole my thunder, but I couldn't pinch her or anything in front of the teacher. And besides, I wanted to know the answer. "She was great!" She said, "That's why I'm a teacher."

After supper, Mrs. Voorhees and my parents went into the living room to visit. Barb and I were to do the dishes. We did not fight about who had to wash and who got   to dry, and we worked quickly so we could go into the living room and listen. We knew better than to talk when adults were talking, but I had so many questions I wanted to ask, most of them about my standing in the first grade. When the evening was over, we all said good night and went to our beds. I slept quite well, even though the teacher was sleeping one floor below me. In the morning, we had pancakes for breakfast even though it was not Saturday, and then we all went off to school. I thought maybe I could ride with Mrs. Voorhees in her car, but my dad said I could not. When we got to school, we pretended like nothing had happened.

Chapter 23: Marjorie Regan Lageson

When I think of Marjorie Lageson, I often think of the picture of George Washington, a standard elementary school-issued portrait of our first president. I remember looking at it a lot, as the picture was dream-like around the edges, as if George was floating on a cloud, but in the middle, his face was all business, determined, yet kind, intelligent, and dignified.

Mrs. Lageson's go-to expression was quite similar. She, too, had a square jaw and an air of dignity about her that was kind, but also straightened students' backs and brought them to attention without saying one word. She taught at the school from 1949-1952. She lived with her husband and three young children in Benson, Minnesota, a town 11 miles east of the school.

Because of the severity of the winters, she spent the week with her in-laws, who lived in the old Regan farmhouse across the road from the school. On Sunday nights, her husband Buck and their children Bob, who was 5, Diane, 3, and baby Kay would drive her to the Lageson farm to spend the week. Bob remembers it being quite difficult to say goodbye to his mother for a long 5 days. She often wrapped a special treat for him in a white handkerchief and told him not to open it until he was back home. He kept his eyes on the handkerchief, gripped in his hand during the long drive to keep from crying.

At times the gravel roads were covered with snowbanks, some 3 to 5 feet tall, formed when the prairie wind whipped up, blowing the snow from the nearby fields onto the road. Any car would find it nearly impossible to make it through. The only choice was to "floor it," which involved depressing the gas pedal all the way to the floor and slamming into the snowbank, hoping to make it to the other side. If you were lucky, the car would "fishtail" back and forth with the force of the engine and make it through to the other side.

One Sunday, as Buck, Marjorie, and the children approached Sport's ditch on the way out to the Lageson farmhouse, a snowbank appeared that was a good 6 feet tall.

It was a monster of a snow drift, taller than the 1943 Chevy. Buck stopped the car, "No way," he said. "I have to get to school," Marjorie said. Without another word, she opened the car door, reached behind the seat for her brown and tan striped suitcase, and said goodbye to Buck and the children. "I don't think this is a very good idea," Buck said, but he knew by the look of determination on his wife's face that it was of no use. Marjorie grabbed the leather handle of her suitcase and started her climb over the snowbank. As she leaned forward to begin the climb, the snow was above her thighs and leaked into her black rubber boots. She continued her climb leaning forward until her weight found solid snow, but she ended up crawling on her hands and knees, dragging her suitcase behind her. Her family watched her until she disappeared down the other side. "See you Friday!" Buck yelled at the snowbank. Marjorie crawled over 3 lesser snowbanks during the 2-mile walk to the farmhouse. Her face and legs were frostbitten, and her toes were ice by the time she arrived on the porch of the farmhouse. "My Lord and Savior," her mother-in-law Amelia said. "How on earth did you get here?" "I walked from Sport's Ditch," she said.

Marjorie had a gift for teaching that went deep. Without saying so, you knew she was in charge. She loved her work and made you love it too. She was a natural. We all knew she would do what she had to do to get the job done.

Marjorie went on to teach for 40 more years, moving to teach in the town school after the country school closed. When she died on Sept. 23rd, 2002, at 83, her funeral at St. Francis Church in Benson was attended by an outpouring of former students. Over 30 floral arrangements were delivered with cards stating, "Your 4th-grade class of 1954," "Your 6th Grade class of 61," all echoes of the gratitude we felt for her and her commitment to us.

Chapter 24: Jeanette Reardon Wetzel

Miss Reardon taught at District 20 from 1954 until 1956. I interviewed her by telephone for this story. At 83, she was living alone in her own home in Washington state. Her husband, Bill, died in 2014, and her five children are all married with lives of their own.

Miss Reardon described enjoying her time teaching in the country school very much. She had been prepared with nine months of teacher's normal school training and was thrilled she got a job that paid $300 dollars a month.

Miss Reardon was my 2nd and 3rd grade teacher. I believed her to be a magical person. Her voice was calm and soothing, and she did not yell at us. She had an easy laugh, and it often seemed that she was having a good time being the teacher. Miss Reardon did not walk across the room, she floated. She smelled clean, like good soap, and she wore very neat blouses that had been pressed and starched, most often white.

I embarrassed myself on more than one occasion by calling her "mama." When that happened, I wished that the wooden floor would open up and swallow me whole. Oh, to be so like a baby, to mistake the teacher for my mama in front of everyone. I knew I had gone overboard in my infatuation with Miss Reardon when rumblings of me being the teacher's pet were floating around, but I had a painful crush.

Like Mrs. Voorhees, my first-grade teacher, I imagined that perhaps it would be possible that Miss Reardon too, would be stranded at school in a snowstorm. Or that her 10-year-old Chevy might break down on a bitterly cold winter day, and she would be stuck at school. I imagined when my father came to pick us up, he would say to Miss Reardon, "You'd better stay with us tonight, and we'll try to get it started tomorrow." I imagined that Miss Reardon would sit next to me in the back seat, and my heart would race with excitement. I imagined she would also sit next to me at supper and that I would show her my baby sister, the barn cats, and the new baby pigs. We would play rummy and old maid after dinner, and we would laugh a lot. I knew Miss

Reardon would have to sleep on the couch because there were no extra beds, but I would give her my pillow. I would fall asleep thinking about my teacher sleeping downstairs, and I would hope her car never started.

Miss Reardon recalled that we were generally well-behaved, but I remember a day that I wish we could take back. Wadded-up paper balls were flying through the air, boys were sword fighting with rulers, leaping over desks, and turning over the recitation table to be used as a bunker. The girls were leaping in the air, flinging themselves off the top of the teacher's desk while screaming "Geronimo, here I come!" Someone had written "Kilroy was here" in large letters on the blackboard. Miss Reardon had gone to the outhouse. Lucy had been assigned the duty of watching for the teacher to open the door to the outhouse and begin her slow walk back to the school. That would give us plenty of time to pick up the debris, erase the blackboard, and turn the desks right side up. Everyone would be seated and working industriously when the door opened. But this time, Lucy got distracted watching the ruler-sword fights and missed Miss Reardon's exit from the toilet. She was on the steps when Lucy saw her from her post at the window.

"Here she comes!" Lucy hissed. "Here she's here," Miss Reardon said. The schoolroom was in shambles, desks lay on their sides, and a pile of chairs was tipped over in the corner. Wads of crumpled paper were scattered everywhere, and the boys were not in their seats. "Kilroy" was still on the blackboard. The silence was deadly. Miss Reardon said nothing. With heads low, the room was returned to order. "Now," Miss Reardon said in a sad voice, "I want you each to take a sheet of paper from your tablet and write what you think your consequences should be." It was the worst possible punishment.

In the summer of 1955, Miss Reardon got a job working at Yellowstone National Park in Montana. There she met Bill Wetzel, a handsome forest ranger, and although she returned to the country school to teach for a second year, the handsome ranger had stolen her heart, and they married the following summer. She invited her students to the wedding, and we felt as though we were being allowed to take part in a fairy tale as we said goodbye to our beloved Miss Reardon.

Chapter 25: Margaret Nagler Voorhees

On a beautiful May Day with the lilacs in full bloom, I visited Mrs. Voorhees, my first-grade teacher, at her home. At 92, she lived alone on her family farm, where she had been   for the past 69 years. The farm is located in Swift County, 12 miles from Benson, Minnesota, the county seat. The last half of the drive was on gravel roads, where the loose gravel can throw an inexperienced driver into the ditch when not careful. I managed to remember that and slow down.

I was unsure what to expect as I hadn't seen Mrs. Voorhees for 68 years. I was greeted by a sturdy white-haired woman with a strong, full voice. She had a clear vitality about her, and she moved comfortably. "You look like your mother," she said. "You look like you," I said. And she did, the same eyes, the same quiet sureness, and dignity. We sat in her kitchen, which was simple and functional, a place where you got things done.

We had little difficulty finding a rhythm for conversation. We both were most enthusiastic talking about farm life, and in particular, birthing calves. We had both seen breech births and discussed the strength it took to assist in a difficult delivery. She was a full-fledged farmwife. She trucked sick cows to the veterinarian, fed cattle, hauled manure, kept a large garden, and fed hungry men.

She was matter of fact in discussing her teaching experience. She was not overly sentimental; she knew her job and how to do it. "Like all things in life, you did what needed to be done," she said. One year of teacher training was her preparation to be a country schoolteacher. She did take classes during the summer, however, and had nearly completed a 4-year degree.

As a teacher, Mrs. Voorhees was fair, even, and organized. She meant business. I don't believe she had any discipline problems because it was clear from day one what was expected, and there did not appear to be much room for testing the limits. We knew what we had to do, and we did it. She had a warm, delightful smile; her eyes smiled too. I did all I could to earn that approving smile. I put my head down and worked, trying not to drift. Mrs. Voorhees and my only classmate Cynthia were prepared and organized, and by swimming upstream against my nature, I could be too. Our first-grade team advanced quickly. We started school in September, and we had finished first grade by Christmas break. We began second grade in January.

Each day after lunch, Mrs. Voorhees took time to read to us from a Laura Ingalls Wilder book. It gave us time to settle down after lunch and get our minds tracking for the second half of the day. I loved the stories and couldn't wait for story time each day. I remember feeling safe and warm as we heard about the hardships of life on the prairie.

Somehow, Mrs. Voorhees managed to teach eight grades every day, including daily lessons in reading, arithmetic, spelling, and history classes. In addition, she swept the floor, washed the blackboards, and fired up the oil burner stove every day.

Mrs. Voorhees taught school for 12 years before retiring to become a full-time farmer's wife, and mother of her two sons. She enjoyed teaching but her life, she said, belonged to the farm.

Citizens of the Month

Don Andersen

Bill Kepner

Mrs. Lageson
(teacher)
SEPTEMBER

Delores Peerboom
OCTOBER

Ray Geyer
NOVEMBER

John "Jack" Green
DECEMBER

Millie Hagrud
JANUARY

I pledge allegiance to the flag of the United States of America, and to the republic for which it stands. One nation, indivisible, with liberty and justice for all.

Roger Geyer
FEBRUARY

Mary Peerboom
MARCH

Jean Kepner
APRIL

Kathy Andersen
MAY

Lucy Ollendick
JUNE

This placard and the individual pictures furnished with the compliments of NATIONAL SCHOOL STUDIOS

Circa 1951 ~ District #20 Country School Students ~ Tara Township ~ Swift County

Chapter 26: Students

While memories of my country school experience fill the lion's share of the pages of this book, I wanted to include in this work the memories of other students who attended District 20 as well.

While visiting the Swift County Historical Society, and with the help of the Director, Reverend Gary Mills, I was able to find the school census reports of 1944, 1946, and 1948. These reports listed the names of all the children who were living in the district up to 21 years of age. The students that I was able to locate were at the school during the 1940s and 1950s. Those students who were there in the 1940s were able to share experiences and stories from earlier years that were most different from mine.

I was able to interview 12 students who had attended District 20. I would have liked to talk with everyone, but the school closed 64 years ago, and we have lost many. Hopefully, the stories below help paint the picture of these bygone years and bring life to those memories.

Along with the former students I interviewed in person, I was able to do telephone interviews with these former students: Catherine Kepner, Delores Peerboom, Pat Kepner, Dick Doyle, Judy Andersen, and Jon Scott Buyck. I was struck by the level of enthusiasm they shared for this project.

Catherine Kepner remembered her friendships with the Acker girls. She clearly remembers her sister Barbara pushing her down the haystack, breaking her leg when she was to begin first grade.

Delores Peerboom remembered the horses that her father Ted harnessed to take her and her sisters to school on cold, snowy days.

Pat Kepner remembers the kittenball game where he slugged the ball straight into my sister Barb's face who was the pitcher.

Judy Andersen remembers her classmate, Rita: "We were attached at the hip," she said. "Rita had endless energy; she never walked; she always ran. Bruce and Scott Kent used to chase us with garter snakes and try to put them down our backs. I am afraid of snakes to this day."

Dick Doyle attended District 20 only one year but hung onto his report cards for all these 64 years. He also recalled that all his classmates are deceased long before their time.

Jon Scott has his own chapter because of his many stories.

I was unable to interview Bill Kepner, Jack Greene, Ray Geyer, Millie Hagerud, Lucy Ollendick, Peter Ollendick, Mike Doherty, Pat Doherty, Linda Doyle, Bruce Kent, Scott Kent, Arnold Kent, and Dale Andersen. They were strong and vital members of our school in the decade of the 1950s. They have all passed and left big holes in the fabric of our community.

Chapter 27: Donald Andersen

My first interview was with Don. He attended the school from 1944 until 1951. As I drove to his home in Melrose that May morning, the Minnesota farmland was decked out in its full spring attire. Grasses were bright green and moving in the ditches, and the wheat and oats were beginning to green up in the fields. When I arrived at Don's home, he was at the door to meet me. At 83, he still had the lanky build of a baseball pitcher, more than 60 years since he had played in college. There was a nasal quality to his speech that reminded me of his mother, Annie, a sturdy and determined woman. She was the mother of eight children and she knew how to stretch a dollar.

He had an authority and presence about him that I had not seen when he was a skinny adolescent working for my father in the hayfields. Don had a long and prestigious career in education, serving as a superintendent of schools for a large swath of central Minnesota. He shared some stories of his country school years.

Sometimes Donnie rode his horse Duke to school. When his sister Kathy was old enough, their father, Woody, grabbed Kathy under her arms and swung her up behind Donnie.

At 10, Donnie could saddle Duke and get him ready for the 2-mile trip to school. Duke was a brown chestnut with a darker brown mane and tail, with soft brown, kind eyes. He didn't like being ridden much, preferring to stay in the pasture and spend his day eating grass and keeping track of the cows. Duke pranced and balked a little when Donnie saddled him. He climbed on Duke's back from the wooden gate that gave him the height he needed to mount him. "Easy, Duke," he laughed as he grabbed the reins. Donnie knew that Duke would settle down once they started moving, and he loved being in charge of the big, old horse.

"Hang on, Kathy!" he shouted back to his sister as they trotted off. It had rained, so the road was muddy. Donnie decided the ditch looked drier, so he headed Duke down the steep bank. As they bounced down into the ditch, Kathy fell off. "I told you to hang on!" Donnie yelled at Kathy. She burst into tears, "My butt is all wet!" she cried. Donnie reached down and was able to drag his sister back up onto the horse. "You better not tell Dad." Back up on the road, Duke plowed through the mud until they reached the school. Mrs. Boettcher came out and lifted Kathy off Duke's back. "You are soaking wet," she said.

Donnie took Duke across the road to Julius Lageson's barn, where Duke spent the school day, and put some oats in the trough in front of him. "You really got me in trouble, Duke," he said. He walked back to the schoolhouse and saw Kathy warming her backside in front of the stove.

"Now, Donald," Mrs. Boettcher said, "Perhaps you can tell me why Kathy is so wet?"

It was the fall of 1949 and deer hunting season. At 11, Donnie was old enough to hunt with his dad, Woody. His grandfather, Sport McDonald, had given Donnie his old bow and a handful of arrows as Sport was too old now to walk the cornfields. "Be careful with that," Sport said, "It isn't a toy." Woody and Sport felt that Donnie would do less damage with a bow than a 12-gauge shotgun at his age. Donnie practiced by shooting arrows into a target he nailed into a straw bale.

Donnie decided to bring his bow with some arrows to school; he was proud of this step into manhood. "This is a real bow!" he said. "I'm going to get a deer this year." "That's not real," Richie Acker said and grabbed it. Donnie took it back and said, "Here, I'll show you." He placed an arrow from his quiver onto the bowstring and pulled back with all his might. He meant to launch the arrow high into the sky between the cottonwoods in the schoolyard, but his finger slipped, and he got Richie on the side of the head. Ritchie fell to the ground, gushing blood from the left side of his face and screaming. Alice ran inside and got Mrs. Boetcher and she found a clean rag and held it to Richie's bleeding face. "I'm taking Ritchie home," she said. "Alice, you are in charge." Donnie fell to the ground sobbing, "I didn't mean to!" he wailed. As it turned out, Richie was okay. But Donnie never forgot.

Don went on to earn an advanced degree in School Administration and ended his career as Superintendent of a large Midwestern school system. After he retired, Don and his wife Kay did volunteer work for The International Executive Services Corporation, and spent several years in Hungary, Egypt, and Namibia, helping to develop and enhance the educational systems in these countries. Now in his eighties, Don has lived his life believing in the power of education to change lives, and he has given hope to many as hope was given to him.

Chapter 28: Alice Peerboom Berres

On a pleasant summer day in June, I visited Alice at her home on Kildare Street in Benson, Minnesota. Alice was a young and vital 86-year-old. Because of the Covid virus, she was on leave from her job as a cook at Sandy's restaurant.

Alice had many memories from her country school years. She remembers walking to school and hurrying her younger sister Delores along. "I had her run between the first set of telephone poles and walk between the next set all the way to school, poor Delores," she chuckled. Alice remembered that the older students helped the younger ones with reading. "I taught Billy Kepner and Richie Acker how to read," she recalls.

In the winter, there was often a patch of ice by the coal shed. "We would take turns running and sliding across it," she recalls. "Once I fell and cut my lip open. Marlys Fennell patched me up when we got back inside the school."

Alice remembered the Acker family well. They had 16 children and there was one in every grade. "Joanie, one of the older ones, was a big husky girl," she said. The father, Frank Acker, butchered cows for the farm families in the area. As payment, he was often given the internal organs, brains, heart, tongue, and liver, to take home to feed his large family. "The Acker kids brought organ meats in their dinner pails to eat. The dinners were very smelly," Alice recalled. "I was very shy, and Joanie would want to trade dinners with me. I was too afraid to say no. I couldn't eat her dinner, so I went hungry." When Alice got home, her mother, Nina, would be upset with how stinky her dinner pail smelled.

In winter, the kids used to sled from the ash pile by the plum trees down toward the outdoor toilets. One day, Lawrence Acker didn't see the barbed wire fence that was partly covered with snow in his path. His eye was bloodied as he struck the barbed wire, and he was taken home. He never received medical care for his injury and ended up losing the sight in his eye.

"My favorite holiday was Halloween because the outdoor toilets would be tipped over; no one knew who did it, but I suspect it was the Fennell and the Acker boys," she recalled. "We would have the next day off from school while the school board put the toilets back up."

Alice was a lively interviewee, and she had a remarkable recall of her school days some 75 years ago. She went on to recover from her shyness, and raised 10 children, and served the community as a cook in a number of local restaurants.

Chapter 29: Mary Lou Peerboom Sachs

I visited Mary Lou in her cozy home on South Nelson Avenue in Appleton, Minnesota. Like her older sister Alice, at age 79, she had an excellent memory. We talked about how she and her family came to live in Tara township. Her grandfather was an immigrant from Holland, she said. He had accumulated wealth in land ownership around Danvers, Minnesota. He gave her father, Ted, and each of his children a farm when they married. As payment, they were required to pay 1/3 of their crops to him until it was decided that they had paid enough.

When she started school, she loved her first-grade teacher Mrs. Boettcher, whom she described as very motherly. She particularly remembered that Mrs. Boettcher had a bed in the school in case she got snowed in. "I don't believe it ever got so bad that she stayed," Mary said, "But she had it there just in case."

Mary remembered a feature of the schoolhouse that I had forgotten. There was a bump on the floor that was raised about 2 inches like a mole burrow that ran the length of the school; desks needed to be placed on either side of the bump in order to be stable. I imagine there was a problem with the foundation that was never addressed. We accepted the bump like all the other bumps in our lives; it was what it was. We learned to live with it, as we   learned to live with many things when you don't have a lot of money: homemade haircuts, hand-me-down clothes that were a little too big or a little too small, cuts and bruises that did get better on their own most of the time.

Mary Lou remembered recess, playing ball outside, and that her nemesis was Richie Acker, who she described as a bully. "You had to stay away from him," she said. In discussing the school day, Mary was most fond of art class. She remembers learning practical skills like how to hem a dress, and how to do embroidery. She recalls Jack Greene showing her how to move the needle and thread through the fabric to make a solid hem.

Mary Lou remembered school lunches and stated that "I can't stand a sandwich nowadays," after eating them for 7 years in her dinner pail. She recalls doing chores both at school and at home. Along with many of the former students I interviewed, she said that pumping water to drink and for hand washing was the hardest job. At home, she fed the chickens and geese, and gathered the eggs. Mary Lou and her father, Ted, milked the cows by hand.

Mary Lou lives alone in her home in Appleton, Minnesota. Her husband, Merlyn, has died. She raised 5 children and worked in her community.

Chapter 30: Katherine Andersen Wente

I traveled down Interstate 35 South to Faribault, Minnesota to interview Kathy who lived with her husband, Robert, in a pleasant home on First Street. Both Robert and Kathy greeted me at the house, and we easily fell into a most enjoyable conversation.

Kathy's first recollections of the school were of her teachers. She loved her first-grade teacher, Mrs. Lageson. She also remembers being especially fond of her 5th and 6th-grade teacher, Miss Reardon. We both remembered a spectacular event that happened after Kathy had completed the 6th grade. All the country school students were invited to Miss Reardon's wedding. We were thrilled to be included. We were awe-struck by her forest ranger husband, Bill, who visited Miss Reardon at school before the wedding. He wore cowboy boots and was quite an exotic and dashing leading man for our daydream stories about our teacher. Kathy recalls hugging Miss Reardon on her wedding day and crying her eyes out because she was moving to Montana with her new husband. She wrote to Miss Reardon for a time after she moved. That summer, Kathy suffered an appendix attack and landed in the hospital for surgery. She wrote to Miss Reardon, who surprised her by mailing her a gift. "I will always remember that," she said.

Kathy remembers learning to read with Mrs. Lageson and her classmate Lucy. "It was so exciting to be able to read a book," she remembers. "The library at the school seemed huge at the time, it was just two bookcases in the corner, but that was enough for us." She also remembers music class, especially the songs the Little Brown Church in the Vale and the Battle Hymn of the Republic as all-time school favorites. Like all of us, Kathy did chores at school and also at home.

Across the road from their farm was a fishing hole formed by a dredged-out ditch that had been created to drain water from the neighboring farms after deluge rain. The pond was named after her grandfather and was known in the community as Sport's ditch. It contained northern pike and bullheads, and was the source of hours of entertainment for both children and adults. "I was afraid of that ditch," she said. "I was scared I would fall in, sink to the bottom, and never come up." "We could always get fish, though," she said. "Sometimes we didn't have much to eat, but we could always go there and bring home fish for supper."

Kathy's farm was two miles from school, and the walk was difficult for her and her brother and sisters. In the early spring, the gravel road would be frozen and easy to walk on in the morning, but by evening the road would be thawed from the spring sun, and the walk home would be in ankle-deep mud. Her family farm was on low land that often flooded in heavy rain, covering their fields and the gravel road. If Kathy's parents were not at the school to pick them up, they were told to start walking home. "One day was particularly difficult," she remembers. "The clay mud sucked our boots off, leaving us muddy, cold, and wet in our stocking feet. Our legs were frost-bitten, and Mary and I were both crying, exhausted from walking, and struggling to put one foot in front of the other. Then we saw dad swerving and grinding through the deep mud in his old pick-up. We were rescued at last."

Kathryn married Robert, her childhood sweetheart, and they raised three children in Faribault, Minnesota. She had a successful career as a manager at the Faribault School for the Deaf.

Chapter 31: Mary Andersen Rasmussen

I visited Mary and her husband, Arnie, at their home in Robbinsdale, a first-ring suburb of Minneapolis, Minnesota. Mary remembers growing up on the farm that once belonged to her grandparents, Sport and Mary McDonald. Her parents, Woody and Annie, bought out Annie's two sisters, Millie and Jeanie after the parents died.

Neither Mary's experience at the country school nor her childhood had been easy. Miss Nagler, her 2nd grade teacher, did not pass her. She joined Barb, Pat, and Gloria to repeat the second grade. In a subsequent interview with Miss Nagler, now Mrs. Voorhees, she said, "Mary was plenty smart, but she was always sick and missed too much school, so I felt I should keep her back."

Mary and her sister Kathy slept in the attic of their small farmhouse. It was not insulated and was very cold in the winter. Mary remembers seeing frost on the nail heads that held the attic together. She remembers always being cold at home and in school; she believed the school wasn't insulated either. "I had double pneumonia that lasted a long time," she said.

Mary told me that her family raised chickens, which were a major source of food and income when times were tight. She was often in charge of making meals for the family and remembers changing from her school clothes to her work clothes and heading down to Sport's ditch to catch some northerns for supper. Mary also caught chickens, expertly chopped off their heads, and cleaned and cooked them for the family's evening meal.

Her father, Woody, played first base on the town baseball team, and Mary said the family spent every Sunday watching him play. During the game, she and her siblings collected pop bottles for spending money, played, and took naps under the bleachers until the game was over.

A school memory Mary recalls fondly happened in the spring of 1958 when she was a sixth grader. That year, we celebrated Minnesota's 100-year centennial. A gathering was planned for all the Swift County schools in Holloway, a neighboring town with a school auditorium. The bunny hop was a featured act in the program. As dance moves were required, tryouts were held. Mary was one of three students from District 20 selected to perform the bunny hop. Her mother made her costume, including ears and a fluffy pink tail. Mary's eyes lit up when she described being selected, the bunny costume, and doing the hop. She recalled that one of her classmates, Pat Kepner, also chosen to bunny hop, lost his bunny tail during the vigorous hopping, and the tail bounced around wildly behind him during the dance.

Mary and her husband, Arnie, adopted a son and raised him to adulthood. They now enjoy their grandchildren. Mary was a talented hairdresser and was in demand from her older sister Kathy and the neighbor Mable Tollefson to keep their hair looking good. She had a successful career as a hairdresser in her adult life.

Chapter 32: Rodger Geyer

I interviewed Rodger at Key's restaurant in Spring Lake Park, Minnesota, on a rainy spring day. As we found each other in the parking lot, I would have known him anywhere. He had an easy way about him, a man who knew hardships and hard work and expected no less. He still had the feel of a prairie man, accustomed to hard weather and strong winds, but sure in his ability to navigate through what had been handed to him. We settled in with coffee and I realized I was peppering him with questions. I took a breath, slowed down and waited; that worked better.

Rodger was in a class with Jean Kepner and Mary Peerboom. In 1955, he completed 6th grade at District 20 and went on to Benson High School. Rodger recalls his country school experience as "getting by " and that he was glad to be done with it. His favorite school activity was kittenball; he had to bat with one hand, so his classmates would not have to chase the ball over the road and into the ditch on the other side.

Rodger became a successful businessman in his adult life. He currently owns a trucking company, and at 80, he continues to actively operate his company with ten dump trucks, contracting with commercial and government construction operations. He owns the family farm in Tara township, as his brother Raymond and his parents Larry and Cele are deceased.

Rodger is the only student who attended District 20 who still owns land there. We would never have thought that the land on which we lived, worked, and went to school would no longer be owned by us. We were a community with a strong heartbeat; we were connected by our school and by our common purpose. We felt that, like the cottonwoods that shaded us, we were rooted there for a lifetime.

Chapter 33: The Dohertys

Two of my sisters, Barb and Helen, attended District 20 with me, along with my two brothers, Mike and Pat. My two youngest sisters, Eileen and Sharon, were not of school age when the school closed in 1959. We were a typical Irish clan, and as such, we watched out for each other.

When Helen was 5 years old and in the first grade, she was being tested on her spelling words by Miss Reardon. Helen wrote down her spelling words on a scrap of paper and kept them beside her spelling worksheet in case she forgot how to spell any of the words. Miss Reardon caught her with her list and marched over and put a big red F on the top of Helen's worksheet. She told Helen she would be staying after school. We were all horrified as Helen sat scared and ashamed at her desk, waiting for her punishment. Barb, Mike, and I stood outside the window lined up in a row glaring at the teacher, waiting for Helen's sentence to expire. When she was released, we marched home, mad. Much later, Helen recalled the incident, "At the age of 5, I had no idea that I was supposed to memorize my spelling words, and it seemed only sensible to have a checklist."

In the spring of her 1st-grade year, Barb remembers feeling weak and tired. She fell behind on the walks home, and she could not keep up with Lucy, Jean, and Pat. At the annual field day held for all the county schools in the spring, she was not able to make her legs move fast enough to run in the races. The morning following field day, she could not get out of bed. Our father rushed her in to see Dr. Griffin who diagnosed her with rheumatic fever. Barb was hospitalized. I was frightened to see my parents so scared. That night, we all knelt on the floor in the living room and prayed the rosary for Barb's recovery. She did get better but had to spend the summer after first grade in bed. At 7, she felt ashamed that she could not help on the farm during the busiest season, and that Daddy had to carry her to mass on Sundays. Mama put our baby sister Eileen in bed with Barb while she was busy with farm work, and they took care of each other.

My brother Mike was not alive to be interviewed. He died of cardiac arrest playing in a volleyball tournament at age 36. I can tell you that he was mature beyond his years and a great student, especially in math and science. I stood between Mike and Cynthia Buyck during spell downs. On Fridays, the 5th and 6th graders lined up at the front of the room along side the recitation table. We spelled the words that our teacher, Mrs. Suter, carefully pronounced for us. If a word was misspelled, down you went back to your desk. Mike and Cynthia never sat down until the teacher ran out of words. They were chosen to represent our school at the county spelling bee. I wished that I could remain standing just once; I even tried crossing my fingers behind my back for luck. It never happened.

My brother Pat was also not interviewed. He died at age 21 in a construction accident. He attended 1st through 3rd grades at the country school. Of his four classmates, born in 1950, the only one who remains is Bob Peerboom. Linda Doyle (Staton) and Bruce Kent have also passed. Pat was born with birth defects. He had ear, wrist, and thumb deformities that required multiple surgeries to correct. Pat had marked hearing loss in his right ear, and his right thumb was not opposable. He adapted remarkably well and asked for no special treatment and was not given any. Pat was born with strong mechanical ability. At age 3, he took apart the crib he slept in and told our mother he was ready for a big bed. The small country school was a great environment for him. He was not special; he was a regular boy whose physical differences were a matter of fact. He was not bullied; woe be it to anyone who tried to do so with 4 older siblings at his elbow. He had a charismatic personality and loved music and fun, especially entertaining with his big brother. His life's dream was to own a nightclub near where our country school is located. I wish he could have lived his dream.

Grief and tragedy have always been a part of the air I breathe. Having a safe, predictable school experience as part of a larger safe, predictable community, and being known, loved, and accepted has made it possible for me to live with the pain that life brings.

Chapter 34: Cynthia Buyck Chua

I visited Cynthia at her home in North Oaks, Minnesota, a gated, private community. It was originally a farm owned by James J. Hill, a railroad magnate, who ironically was the prime mover in settling immigrants in Tara Township, where Cynthia was raised and attended District 20 school. Cynthia's home was large, modern, and well-appointed. She invited me in, and we began reminiscing about our childhood experiences.

Cynthia recalls that her parents came to Tara township from Tracy, Minnesota, in Lyon County to buy a farm. The Buycks needed a farm they could afford. Soil in southern Minnesota was richer and priced higher than the land in Tara township.

Throughout Cynthia's childhood, the family worked hard to improve the land and to pay off the mortgage. Farm life was grueling work. It required picking rocks from the field in order to keep the farm machinery from breaking, carrying food and water to the farm animals, and long hours planting, cultivating and harvesting, always with an eye on the weather. The grain needed to be planted before the rains turned the fields into a muddy swamp, and harvested before a hailstorm thundered in across the prairie and shredded the crop. They stood vigil for an early freeze that would end the crop's life.

Because her mother needed to help in the fields and care for the animals, Cynthia was in charge of the house and her younger brothers. She recalls making supper and that all the food was made from scratch. Her mother bought the basics at the Red Owl grocery in town, flour, sugar, salt, pepper, and margarine. The family had their own beef, pork, chicken, eggs, and milk. Fruit and vegetables that the garden gave up in the spring and summer were both enjoyed and preserved to be used in the winter.

When I visited Cynthia's house, I felt the discipline that was present the minute I walked in the door. Her home was clean, tidy, organized, and quiet. Comparatively, our house was a circus; chaotic, messy, warm, and overflowing with talking, yelling, and laughing. Our school behavior mirrored our home life. Cynthia's desk was organized, her pencils sharpened, and her books and tablet in their proper places. My desk was a jumble of books, papers, and broken leaded pencils. Like my grandfather, I spent too much time imagining various scenarios where I would be the hero, saving everyone from the burning school or hitting the ball over into the ditch and speeding around the bases, touching home, victorious. Cynthia, on the other hand, lived in the present.

My saving virtue was competition, and I desperately wanted to do better than Cynthia. She brought me along with her high achievement and work ethic. I remember gnawing my broken pencil to get past the wood to the lead so I could write something, tearing through a pile of papers on my desk to find my worksheet, and frantically finishing it as Miss Reardon's footsteps were closing in from behind. I could read, though, and I could tell stories, and we were neck and neck in arithmetic. We finished first grade by Christmas time and started the second-grade reader and spelling book after the break in January.

I loved social studies class. Our textbook, Our World and Its People, told stories about children from all over the world. The stories seemed outlandish to me, more like fairy tales, and I doubted they were true. My life consisted of 5 square miles, school, church, uncles, aunts and cousins, and home. But when I read "The Good Earth" by Pearl Buck at 11, I knew that every word in that book was true and that there was an entire world out there that I knew nothing about.

Cynthia would be at her desk working by the time my siblings and I burst into the school as the teacher was ringing the bell, just under the wire from being tardy. Cynthia typically got a ride to school from her mother, Pearl, but sometimes her parents were busy in the afternoon with farm work, and she needed to walk home.

She had a 2 mile walk that required her to walk past the Hageruds cattle. They were huge white-faced Herefords raised for beef, weighing up to 2,000 pounds each. The cattle would race to the fence line when they saw Cynthia coming, probably more out of curiosity than malicious intent, but she was afraid the fence might not hold. And then, there was the matter of the bull which snorted and pawed the ground, threatening to charge.

Cynthia decided it would be best to stay off the road and walk home through the corn fields. She would choose a row of corn to follow and try to stay on it until she came out by the ditch that was near her farm, well past the Herefords. One might think this choice was the easy one, but in the middle of the corn field, surrounded by an ocean of browning, ripening corn, it became difficult to know north from south, east from west, each stalk of corn identical to the next. A child could easily become lost and disoriented in a forest of corn. But Cynthia never did, and she never told her parents that she had walked through the cornfield. They would not like that.

Cynthia talked about the Christmas program, the highlight of the school year. One year she had gotten into a fight with her brother Jon. He had thrown a plate at her that cut her near her eye. The cut bled mightily and probably required stitches, but in those days, going to the doctor was not something that happened. She remembers reciting a poem for the Christmas program, with a bandage over her face, exclaiming "We never quarrel, we never fight."

Cynthia went on to earn a master's degree in journalism and a master's in business administration. She held executive positions in the communications industry, married, and raised three children. Her husband Ed, a native of Singapore, is retired from a distinguished career as a psychiatrist. I would like to think that some of her interest in journalism is related to the heated competition between us in mastering the written word.

Chapter 35: Keith Kent

I visited Keith Kent at his home, just west of Clontarf, Minnesota, in the fall. Keith was well prepared for the interview, he had thought about his country school years, and had taken notes of his recollections.

"I couldn't wait to get to school," he said. "Our farm was close by, and I had been going past the school for as long as I could remember before I was old enough to go there," Keith recalled his first-grade teacher, Miss Jeanette Reardon. "I really liked her," he said, "I would go early to help her with the chores before school." He got to school on his bike, which was a Christmas present from his parents. He could zip up to the school in under 5 minutes and be home again in record time. Keith loved reading and reciting in school. He was an excellent speaker and went on to be an accomplished storyteller in his community.

Keith remembered school chores. "I did a lot of pumping water," he said. One September, when it was 90 degrees, Miss Reardon asked him to get a fresh pail of water so that after recess everyone could have a drink. As Keith was pumping water, he saw a gopher run into his hole. After pouring three buckets of water down the hole, the gopher appeared at the back hole, and was captured by Peter, who was waiting for him there. The gopher fiercely bit Peter. Keith remembers that the boys all shouted, "Rabies! You are going to get rabies!"

Rabies was a big fear. If you contracted rabies, you would die a horrible death, foaming at the mouth and becoming psychotic and aggressive. We all knew that it was inevitable. Someday your cat or dog will be bitten by a wild animal and would then bite you. In a short time, you would be foaming at the mouth, hallucinating and attacking your family, and would suddenly drop dead. This was one of many medical fears we shared at country school.

Another fear was eating rhubarb or green apples. I can recall a time when Keith was 5 and I was 6; we were out in the trees behind his family's house. We discovered what we believed to be rhubarb, so we ate some. Keith's father, Chuck, found us behind the house and said, "Don't eat that! It's poison and it'll kill you." We said not one word. I went home and went out and sat behind the brooder house, waiting to die. I did not, of course, and life went on.

Besides pumping water at school, Keith remembered chores at home, including milking the cows and carrying pails of feed to them. "I started milking cows when I was 5, but my brother Bruce was the best milker. About two years into milking, I found out his secret. He would dip his fingers in the milk pail, and his milk-slippery fingers would easily strip the milk from the cows' teats," Keith said.

Keith felt like he got a good education at the country school. "Those were the glory days," he said. "They were some of the best years of my life."

Keith had an accomplished career as a welder and was known to be able to do welding work above and beyond the ability of others in his field. He and his wife Marlene raised two children on the original Kent homestead and continue to live in the community.

Chapter 36: Ronald Kent

In the summer, I visited Ron Kent at his home on the outskirts of Clontarf, Minnesota. Upon entering Ron's yard, I was overwhelmed by his immense garden, row upon row of every vegetable imaginable. Abundant tomato plants, cucumbers, onions, and garlic stretched out into the field that he carefully tended behind his home. We toured the garden in Ron's golf cart and then went inside to talk about the country school days.

He remembered his first day of school. Ron's father, Dave, had said, "Why don't you stay home and farm with me?" Ron thought that sounded like a pretty good idea. When his mother, Cele, brought him to school, he didn't want to stay. She finally gave up and brought him home again. His father ended up bringing him back to school, making sure that he knew that staying home and farming at age 5 was not an option.

Ron remembers the winter-time school lunches with potatoes and soup cooking on the oil burner stove, and how great they smelled and tasted.

One year in the fall, after a hard rain, the water in the ditch directly across the road from the school froze. The boys had a great time on the ice until someone fell through. Ron wasn't sure which boy fell through, but he does remember the boy sitting by the oil burner stove drying his socks and shoes.

One of Ron's classmates, Peter, was a wild child. He had a shock of red hair and freckles peppered his face. Miss Reardon eventually lost patience with Peter and prepared to crack his knuckles with her wooden ruler. We all knew Peter was in trouble. It was a solemn occasion as no corporal punishment had been meted out before. Miss Reardon's face was red, and her voice was shaky. She brought the ruler down over Peter's extended hands. As the ruler came down, Peter deftly pulled his hands away. "You stop that, Peter!" Miss Reardon shouted. Back and forth they went, Miss Reardon swinging the ruler, Peter snatching his hands away. This dance continued for what seemed like an eternity but was probably a minute or less. Giving up, Miss Reardon said, "Now, Peter, you will stay after school for one-half hour." This was the only attempt at corporal punishment we could remember. For the most part, we were all obedient and respectful of the teacher. But Peter had red hair, which couldn't be helped.

Besides doing chores at school, Ron remembers chores after school on the farm. He fed and milked the cows and cleaned the barns. He knew well the hard work of being a farm boy. Work started at an early age and lasted as long as they were members of the   household. Farm boys spent summers as hired hands for their fathers. One of the jobs, baling alfalfa for cattle feed was hot, grueling work. At times, boys were kept home from school if a crop needed to be harvested quickly because of threatening weather.

Ron learned his work ethic early and continues working hard in his huge garden at 73.

Chapter 37: Jon Scott Buyck

I interviewed Jon by telephone. We laughed a lot during the interview. He reminded me a great deal of his mother, Pearl. They were both intelligent, quick-witted, and engaging. Jon remembers attending District 20 for two years, from 1957 to 1959. He described being "surrounded by women " in his grade and that he enjoyed chasing his classmates, Judy Andersen and Rita Ollendick, around trying to kiss them. He recalls being a fast runner, and that it was hard for the big boys to catch him to teach him a lesson. He told me that he still holds the record for the fastest mile in his high school.

Jon's childhood always involved farm chores. He remembers feeding 1,000 chickens, gathering eggs, and cleaning the barns throughout his childhood. He described school being difficult for him as he was dyslexic, and strategies for dealing with learning disabilities were not well known in the middle 1950s. Jon, however, was persistent and successful in finding his own way to compensate for his dyslexia because of his strong intellect. He graduated from college and went on to succeed in his life's work.

He taught auto mechanics at a suburban high school, worked in risk management for a major insurance company, and was a journeyman carpenter and a construction project supervisor. Currently, Jon runs his own remodeling business.

Jon believes his childhood taught him how to work hard and deal with what life brought his way. He recalls his hands being raw and blistered from cleaning barns and freezing his fingers re-roofing a neighbor's house when they were in need of help. He has learned to accept pain as a part of his life.

Jon describes the students at the country school as the last of a generation who were expected to do what was needed to contribute at home, in school, and in the larger community.

Chapter 38: Last Days

In the spring of 1959, District 20 was closed for good. The decision was made by the school board who were my father, John Doherty, my uncle, Chuck Kent, and our neighbor, Ray Ollendick. It seemed that the board got wind of plans by the Minnesota legislature to force the consolidation of rural state schools that did not operate high schools. The state had maximum leverage as it provided the lion's share of funding to operate the schools. Although the township tax base did provide money for schools, there was no way that Tara Township could carry the school burden alone. At that time too, it was also felt that students would have more opportunities in the larger schools with better-prepared teachers, and programs for art, music, advanced mathematics, and sports. Most of these legal changes occurred during the 1960s, and by 1970, all but three schools in Minnesota had an elementary and secondary program. The country school system had essentially been eliminated. (15)

Our school board saw this coming, and decided to consolidate with the Clontarf school, which was the neighboring village. The village school already had a consolidation arrangement with the high school in Benson, Minnesota, the larger county seat 5 miles south, and were allowed to maintain their elementary school. I speculate that the school board feared we would be pressured to consolidate with Hancock, a Lutheran town, also nearby. We were a Catholic community tied to Clontarf, where we attended church and were a part of the social fabric of that community. I believe all 3 board members were concerned that their combined 19 children might become too cozy with the Lutherans and marry outside the church, which at the time was blasphemous. And so, it was decided we would go to school in Clontarf. I was only a little disappointed. I would be leaving our school after 6th grade anyhow, and a short detour to the Clontarf School for 1 year before attending the high school in Benson seemed reasonable.

We visited the Clontarf school in the spring of 1959 when I was in the 6th grade. I was shocked by the size. The building was 3 stories tall, a substantial brick building. There were 75 students in the school. A bell rang to signal the start and end of school, lunch break, and morning and afternoon recess. There was school lunch; no more potatoes baking on the stove. Alice Amlin, the cook, made delicious baked beans and excellent brownies. George Reardon, the janitor, did all the chores we were used to doing. George was our hero; in addition to taking care of the school, he took care of the students. We fought to sit next to him at lunch time and tried to think up excuses to spend time with him in his room downstairs. George was the father of our beloved Miss Reardon which gave him special powers indeed.

The last picnic that spring was the same as every year. We had races, ate potato salad, chicken, and Rice Krispie bars, and drank orange Kool-Aid. We got our report cards, and everyone passed. No one said, "this is the last picnic." We did not say goodbye to the school room, the plum trees, or each other. It would never be the same. We were excited about something new, and we didn't know what we had lost. In our three-story school, with indoor toilets, running water, and a piano, we had no jobs. We did not pump water, wash blackboards or pound erasers. George, the janitor, did all of that. There were three teachers, and they did not need us to practice reading with the first graders or help the second graders with their arithmetic worksheets.

There was a piano and a stage for the Christmas program. I don't know what happened to our dyed blue sheets strung across the front of the school. There was a merry-go-round but no plum trees. We had to pretend like we were not friends with the boys and say" yuck" if they talked to us. In our country school, we were collaborators, working together to educate everyone. We were necessary. We did our part, and we felt a sense of agency, of responsibility.

The 7th grade classes were surprising. We read aloud, and we suffered with some of the boys as they struggled to read. Our teacher began the year in arithmetic by stating, "this is a percent sign," and writing it on the board. We learned that last year. I looked at Cynthia; it was going to be a long year.

The Clontarf kids were light years ahead of us on one topic. Sex. I knew nothing, and they knew everything. During recess, Beverly would educate me and enjoy my ignorance. "Do you know how babies get born?" I didn't. She told me. I was quite certain that Beverly made the whole thing up. "Who told you that?" I asked. "Sonny, he's done it already," she said. I knew it wasn't true because my parents had 7 children, and they would never have done a thing like that once, let alone 7 times. "Ask the teacher if you don't believe me," Beverly said. "I'm not going to ask her that. It's dumb," I said. Something inside of me felt that she might be right, but I wasn't going to ask Mrs. Lageson or my mother about it. I felt it was probably a mortal sin to talk about such things, and how was I going to tell the priest what I had said?

Chapter 39: Reflections

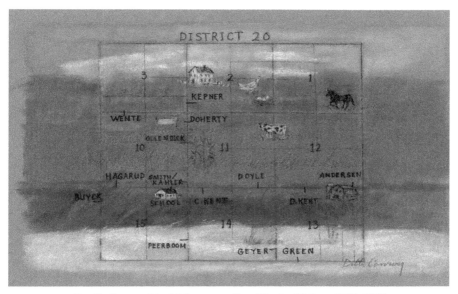

Family farms with children attending District 20 from 1950-1959

And so, as District 20 closed at the end of May 1959, we were looking forward not back. We did not know what we had lost. Our school was the principal thread that bound the community together. It was the place where we learned and grew, the gathering place for the community. We voted there, we held our meetings and celebrations there, and learned to know and care about each other there. We belonged there.

In the 1950s, 14 families with school-age children attended our country school. Currently, there are only 2 families with children attending schools in town. We lost more than a population, we lost the strongest threads that bound us together, that held our common purpose.

We did not say goodbye to our school and to our way of life. We did not know it was over. We were looking forward to the new school, to music classes and hot lunch, more friends, and the school bus.

We can say goodbye now.
The building, though forlorn, still stands,
Our dim, lost memories can be found.
Within a snapshot or an old valentine,

We can remember the time.
We sang, The Little Brown Church and Oh Susanna,
We painted ketchup bottles red for Mother's Day surprises,
We smelled the potatoes baking on the stove,

We can remember when.
We found ourselves in a blizzard with no way forward or back,
We felt the crack of the wooden bat in our hands,
We experienced the excitement minutes before the curtain.

We can remember.
The races, the report cards, the fathers making picnic tables,
The stories read after lunch of Pa, Ma, Laura, Mary and Carrie,
The old books, the new shoes, the water pail, the dinner buckets,
The outdoor toilets, the Big Chief tablets, the wet mittens
The teachers who knew us and cared for us.
The quiet solid feeling of belonging.

Acknowledgments

I am forever grateful to Joyce Gudding who has been at my side editing, encouraging, and providing technical support throughout the writing process.

I am grateful to my coach and editor, Leslie Koepke, who has been instrumental in holding my wandering feet and brain to the fire.   Also, to Christie Getches for editing, marketing savvy, and encouragement.

I have endless gratitude beyond measure to my four sisters:

- Sharon, whose eagle eye on both form and substance, was the last edit.
- Eileen, who holds the pulse of the community, told me stories that contributed to the tone of this book.
- Helen, thank you for the book title, and for constant assurances that I was on the right track.
- Barb, who was my side kick and partner in crime in many of these stories.

I wish to thank Della Conroy for her paintings. Her work added a spiritual dimension to the story that words could never convey.

Also, I want to thank our former teacher, Jeanette Reardon Wetzel who miraculously kept a shoe box full of school photos that brought life to the story.

Sources

In the process of writing this book, I traveled to the Swift County Historical Society several times, and with the guidance of the director, Rev. Gary Mills, I was able to discover a great deal about the early days of our school.

In addition, I was aided mightily by the historical work of Ann Regan, Editor in Chief of the Minnesota Historical Society, whose work helped me to understand the impact of Irish immigration on our Tara township.

Although I drew on a substantial number of resources in writing this book, there were 3 sources that were most helpful:

- Swift County, Minnesota, A Collection of Historical Sketches and Family Histories, Swift County Historical Society Benson, Minnesota, (Taylor Publishing Company, Dallas Texas 1979);
- Irish in Minnesota, by Ann Regan, (Minnesota Historical Society Press, St. Paul Minnesota, 2002);
- MNopedia, an online resource supported by the Minnesota Historical Society.

Endnotes

1. Swift County Minnesota, A Collection of Historical Sketches and Family Histories, Swift County Historical Society, Benson, Minnesota (Taylor Publishing Company, Dallas, Texas 1979) p. 630

2. IBID. page 632

3. IBID page 630

4. IBID page 584

5. IBID page 630

6. Irish in Minnesota, Ann Regan, (Minnesota Historical Society Press,) St. Paul MN. pp. 5-6

7. IBID pp. 5-6

8. IBID p. 8

9. Weber, Eric. "Treaty of Traverse des Sioux, 1851." MNopedia, Minnesota Historical Society. http://www.mnopedia.org/event/treaty-traverse-des-sioux-1851 (accessed May 26, 2023).

10. Sanders, Thomas. "Jeffers Petroglyphs." MNopedia, Minnesota Historical Society. http://www.mnopedia.org/place/jeffers-petroglyphs (accessed May 26, 2023).

11. http://www.startribune.com/softball-started-in-minnesota-or-did-it/429130543

12. Ford, Alyssa. "Children's Blizzard, 1888." MNopedia, Minnesota Historical Society. http://www.mnopedia.org/event/childrens-blizzard-1888 (accessed May 26, 2023).

13. https://www.dnr.state.mn.us/climate/summaries_and_publications/winter_storms.html

14. Swift County, Minnesota, A Collection of Historical Sketches and Family Histories, Swift County Historical Society, Benson, Minnesota, (Taylor Publishing Company, Dallas Texas 1979) page 632

15. www.legislature>HouseofRepresentatives>House Research>Education>SchoolDistrict Consolidations

List of Teachers

When the school was established in 1877, it has been reported that Nellie Knall was the first teacher. After Nellie, there were no records found until 1887.

The following is a list of the teachers from 1887 to 1959, except for 1898 to 1904 when no records could be located. This list was taken from Swift County Minnesota by Swift County Historical Society/Printed 1979.

1887 - J. Delaney
1888 - 1889 - Mary Kelly
1890 - Katie Thornton
1890 - Maggie Duggan
1890 - E.F. McGinnes
1891 - Libbie Fleming
1892 - Ed Patrick
1893 - Maggie Meaghen
1894 - J.J. Piercell
1895 - Theresa Reilly
1896-1897 Maggie Duggan
1898 - 1904 - No records
1905 - Marie Kalkman
1906 - Margie Jennings
1907 - Katherine O'Neill
1908 - Katherine Quinn
1909 - Mae Conlogue.
1910 - 1912 - Margaret Gosson
1912 - Mae Gregory
1914 - Lenora Karrigan
1915 - Jennie Conlogue
1916 - Tillie Pearsons
1917 - Jane Conlogue
1918 - Mae Gallagher

1919 - Marcella Reardon
1920 - Laura Dolan
1921 - Clara Dolan
1922 - 1923 - Marie Connors
1924 - Clara Dolan
1925 - Sylvia Walsh
1928 - 1931 - Catherine Doherty Kent
1931 - Josephine Burke
1932 - 1934 - Marjorie Regan
1935 - Catherine Kent Johnson
1936 - 1937 - Allen Espeset
1938 - Vera Gustafson
1939 - 1940 - Irene Bonnie
1941 - Irene Forbord
1943 - Mary Kent
1944 - Evelyn Knutson
1945 - Mary Kent
1945 - Ida Rowberg
1945 - 1949 - Eva Boettcher
1949 - 1952 - Marjorie Regan Lageson
1952 - 1954 - Margaret Nagler Voorhees
1954 - 1956 - Jeannette Reardon
1956 - 1957 - Joan Arnold
1957 - 1959 - Verona Rekstad Suter

Printed in the USA
CPSIA information can be obtained
at www.ICGtesting.com
JSHW071134280723
45467JS00012B/22

9 781916 622999